D0582072

JUST
Like
DAD
Says

JUST
Like
DAD
Says A BOOK
OF DAD'S
WIT

Geoff Tibballs

EBURY
PRESS

First published in 2009 by Ebury Press, an imprint of Ebury Publishing
A Random House Group company

Collection copyright © Geoff Tibballs 2009

Geoff Tibballs has asserted his right to be identified as the
author of this Work in accordance with the Copyright, Designs
and Patents Act 1988

The Random House Group Limited Reg. No. 954009

Addresses for companies within the Random House Group can
be found at www.randomhouse.co.uk

A CIP catalogue record for this book is available from
the British Library

The Random House Group Limited supports The Forest Stewardship
Council (FSC), the leading international forest certification
organisation. All our titles that are printed on Greenpeace approved
FSC certified paper carry the FSC logo. Our paper procurement
policy can be found at www.rbooks.co.uk/environment

Printed in the UK by CPI Mackays, Chatham, ME5 8TD

ISBN 9780091930479

To buy books by your favourite authors and register for offers visit
www.rbooks.co.uk

In loving memory of my own dear Dad

Contents

Introduction

If the post of dad were to be advertised, it would surely command a six-figure salary. Consider just the basic requirements: financier, jester, chauffeur, peacekeeper (to UN standard), fairground ride, sous chef, lover to partner (seasonal), schoolteacher, agony uncle, encyclopaedia – and all that is after you've passed the physical. It is a job which most men gladly accept despite being spectacularly unqualified – after all, since when did being an expert on lagers of the world and the offside rule prepare anyone for changing a nappy that smells like the inside of a giraffe house?

The one consolation for today's new dads is that at least they have easy-to-use disposable nappies. The old towelling nappies necessitated a degree in advanced geometry as you formed a series of equilateral triangles held together by a giant safety pin, the tip of which could inflict considerable damage on an errant thumb at two in the morning. Even when the complex configuration was complete, there was always a chance that you had accidentally pinned the nappy to the plastic changing mat, with the result that baby would spend the next three hours carrying around an inflatable on its back. Then there was the overpowering stench of the solution into which the soiled nappies were soaked before washing – a reminder if one were needed as to why Hugo Boss has never marketed a men's aftershave with the great scent of ammonia.

Fatherhood is certainly not a chore to be undertaken lightly. The brochure may promise fun-filled family days out at Disneyland or watching your offspring win Wimbledon but the reality is sleepless nights, years of worry, and the expectation that, even at the end of a long working day, you will still be able to build a full-size Lego replica of the Palace of Versailles and identify every Care Bear without hesitation. And anyone who tells you that the first five years are the worst either moved out or sold their child before he or she became a teenager.

It doesn't even end there. Whereas once kids couldn't wait to leave home, now boys in particular flee the nest as readily as an eagle chick with a broken wing and vertigo. Yet in spite of the hardships and sacrifices – waiting an hour to use the bathroom, a quarterly phone bill equal to the national debt of Denmark – we endure it all stoically because deep down we know that there is no greater feeling in the world than being a dad. And to prove it, our bottom drawer is crammed with unworn pairs of socks and hideous ties that not even Elton John would be seen in – tokens of appreciation from Father's Days past.

Becoming a dad

If a man can survive his partner's pregnancy without her making at least one attempt on his life, he can count himself lucky.

A woman's most common craving during pregnancy is for the father to be pregnant.

Anon

My wife just told me the good news – I'm going to be a dad for the first time. The bad news is we already have two kids.

Brian Kiley

Gary doesn't understand periods. He thinks they're something to do with the moon.

Dorothy Bishop, Men Behaving Badly

You should take care of your wife when she's pregnant. Don't say stupid stuff, like me. I came home one time and she's lying on the couch and there's food and clothes everywhere. I walked in and went: 'What did you do today?' My wife looked up and said: 'Today? I don't know. Let's see… what did I do today? Today I made a lung.'

Henry Cho

—I think it'll be a boy.
—I think it'll be a girl.
—Phoebe, you thought Ben would be a girl.
—Have you seen him throw a ball?

Ross Geller and Phoebe Buffay, Friends

Listen, son, I know you're worried about the baby coming, but you don't have to be. Yes, you're not going to be the youngest any more, and it is true the baby will get all of our attention for quite a while, and you will have to do a lot more work around the house, and probably have to share the bedroom…

Hal, Malcolm in the Middle

If this baby's half as bad as our least bad one, we're still ruined.

Hal, Malcolm in the Middle

Why am I excited to become a father? Two words: Swedish nanny.

David Letterman

I'm preparing for the baby. I'm busy putting child-proof caps on all the bottles of booze.

David Letterman

It's never a good idea to ask a woman if she's pregnant. If she's not, you're in huge trouble. I don't care if she's in the delivery room and the baby is halfway out. I would still play it safe and say, 'Excuse me, you've got a little something on your leg there.'

Kevin Nealon, Yes, You're Pregnant, But What About Me?

—Are you alright?
—Well, let's see, everything's twice the size it was nine months ago and I'm growing another head inside me.

Tony Smart and Dorothy Bishop, Men Behaving Badly

Despite the fact you have done nothing these nine months, the baby is 50 per cent you. Some mothers never forgive the father for this.

Marcus Berkmann, Fatherhood: The Truth

Congratulations are in order for Woody Allen – he and Soon Yi have a brand new baby daughter. It's all part of Woody's plan to grow his own wives.

David Letterman

There can be few happier and prouder moments in a man's life (except maybe the first time you manage to pee completely over the urinal at school) than watching your partner desperately squatting over a mirror, legs in two different time zones, face the colour of a blueberry muffin, screaming, between gasps of gas and air, 'I'll get you for this, you evil bastard' and thinking: 'I did that.'

Jeff Green, The A–Z of Having a Baby

My wife was in labour for 32 hours. And I was faithful to her the entire time.

Jonathan Katz

I'm told I'm a 'coach' and my job is to remind my wife to breathe. When was the last time you had to be reminded to breathe?

Robert Klein

By doing a bit of breathing and panting, men have this image that they're sharing the birthing experience. Not unless they're passing a bowling ball, they're not.

Robin Williams

My wife and I traipsed along to natural childbirth classes, breathing and timing. We were a terrific team and had a swell time. The actual delivery was slightly more difficult. I don't want to name names, but I held my end up.

Dave Barry

The old system of having a baby was much better than the new one, the old system being characterised by the fact that the man didn't have to watch.

Dave Barry

What's all this fuss about fathers being present at the birth of their children? The way events are shaping, they'll be lucky to be present at the conception.

George H. Davies

The nurse held me up after the birth and said to Father: 'Here's your son. Eight pounds.' He looked at me and said, 'Make it nine pounds ten and I'll throw his cot in as well.'

Les Dawson

When I was born the doctor came out to the waiting room and said to my father: 'I'm very sorry. We did everything we could…but he pulled through.'

Rodney Dangerfield

Watching a baby being born is a little like watching a wet St Bernard coming in through the cat door.

Jeff Foxworthy

We were well prepared for natural childbirth, which means that no drugs can be given to the female during delivery. The father, however, can have all he wants.

Bill Cosby, Fatherhood

I told my wife I don't want to be there at the birth. I don't see why my evening should be ruined too.

Dennis Wolfberg

They say men can never experience the pain of childbirth. But they can, if you hit them in the goolies with a cricket bat for 14 hours.

Jo Brand

The pain from a kick in the bollocks is worse than the pain from childbirth. How do I know? Because a few years down the line a woman will say to her partner, 'Do you want to try for another baby?' But I have never heard a man say, 'I'd like another kick in the bollocks.'

Jason Manford

She [Nicole Appleton] said having the baby was easier than having a tattoo. I really don't want to know what sort of tattoo parlours she's been to.

Liam Gallagher

For a father a home birth is preferable. That way you're not missing anything on television.

Jeremy Hardy

We have a very active sex life and we both sat down and contemplated over a bottle of wine that it wasn't good for our sexual relationship for me to be at childbirth. I told her I'd feel squeamish seeing that level of mess. It's like sending 25 vegans into a kitchen with meat in the blender.

Gordon Ramsay

I have tremendous respect for women after watching my wife give birth three times. I could never, ever raise a child to whom I gave birth. You know, because a newborn is about the size of a basketball, and if I had to expel a basketball from my body via a very restricted passageway, I would never want to see that basketball again. Not even on weekends.

Jeff Stilson

I mean, look at the fuss women make about childbirth. Now, I'm not saying it doesn't smart a bit, but if blokes did it, I reckon you'd be looking at, what, give birth, have a couple of Paracetamol, maybe a bit of a nap and then back to work within the hour.

Gary Strang, Men Behaving Badly

There are two things in life for which we are never truly prepared: twins.

Josh Billings

If I ever have twins, I'd use one for parts.

Steven Wright

If nature had arranged that wives and husbands should have children alternately, there would never be more than three in a family.

Lawrence Housman

Me and my girlfriend had a lot of rows about the whole baby thing. I've wanted to have a baby for about five years. But she wants to keep it forever.

Lee Mack

—We could have tried for another baby. We could have been a family again.
—I know. That's why I didn't try.

Alma Hodge and Orson Hodge, Desperate Housewives

I used to think there was some sort of mix-up at the hospital when Frasier was born. Of course, when Niles came along, it shot that theory all to hell.

Martin Crane, Frasier

My daughter will want for nothing. She'll have dollies-a-plenty. And bears but no clowns, they scare me.

Jonny Keogh, Two Pints of Lager and a Packet of Crisps

Warren Beatty only had children so he could meet some babysitters.

David Letterman

Being a dad is the new black.

Laurence Llewelyn-Bowen

I love producing children. It's fun! I don't like taking care of children, but I love producing children.

Donald Trump

Most of us become parents long before we have stopped being children.

Mignon McLaughlin

Ideally they should give you a couple of 'practice kids' before you have any for real. Sort of like bowling a few frames for free before you start keeping score. Let you warm up.

Paul Reiser

What's in a name?

Just because celebrities give their children daft names, there is no need for the rest of us to follow suit. Calling your child Bluebell Madonna could create terrible problems in adulthood – particularly if he becomes a docker.

What prompted Gwyneth Paltrow and Chris Martin to name their daughter after a Golden Delicious?

Anon

How would you like to go through life with the name Cooper Banks-Mackenzie? The kid's gonna sound like a law firm.

Matty Banks, Father of the Bride Part II

If we wanted wussies as kids, we would've named them Dr Quinn and Medicine Woman.

Ricky Bobby, naming his boys Walker and Texas Ranger, Talladega Nights

The other day I was served by a girl in Boots called Mmmm…Danone.

Alan Carr

We have two boys. We named them Jackson and Grant. We figured, 'What the heck, they're going to fight anyway.'

Henry Cho

We grew up laughing at Frank Zappa for calling his daughter Moon Unit, but today we're naming our kids after remote Himalayan villages and exotic cheeses.

Jeremy Clarkson, And Another Thing…

I am dull and unimaginative because when I was little, two of my tortoises, Sullivan and Bubble, died. That left me with Gilbert and Squeak, which made me a laughing stock and gave me a profound respect for a sensible naming policy.

Jeremy Clarkson, And Another Thing…

Always end the name of your child with a vowel, so that when you yell the name will carry.

Bill Cosby

I gave my kids normal names, not names like Peaches, Blossom, Autumn, Apple and Cherry – like a range of Glade plug-ins.

Jack Dee

Any child can tell you that the sole purpose of a middle name is so he can tell when he's really in trouble.

Dennis Fakes

Colin is the sort of name you give your goldfish for a joke.

Colin Firth

—Okay, how about Ruth?
—Oh, I'm sorry, are we having an 89-year-old woman?

Rachel Green and Ross Geller, Friends

—Okay, I got one. If it's a girl…Sandrine. It's French.
—That's a great name…for an industrial solvent.

Rachel Green and Ross Geller, Friends

The most common mistake in choosing a name comes from forgetting the fiendish tortures that kids inflict on other kids because of an unconventional name, an unfortunate set of initials, or a cute nickname that becomes less cute with each passing year.

Peter Mayle, How To Be A Pregnant Father

When I was born in 1935 my father wanted me called Melbourne Parkinson because the England cricket team had just won a Test match there.

Michael Parkinson, Parky: My Autobiography

Betty Rubble: Does he have a name?
Adoption Agency Worker: Bamm-Bamm.
Barney Rubble: Is that short for something?
Adoption Agency Worker: Yes, Bamm-Bamm-Bamm.

The Flintstones

You know what was hard for me, coming up with names for our children. I panic when I have to name a new document on my computer. I got so desperate toward the end of my wife's third pregnancy I found myself reading the credits at the end of movies, looking for names – which means at some point I'll have to explain to my little boy that he was named after the key grip on *Dude, Where's My Car?*

Jeff Stilson

—What name have they decided on?
—If it's a girl they're calling her Sigourney after an actress, and if it's a boy they're naming him Rodney after Dave.

Mike and Trigger, Only Fools and Horses

Nappy talk

As a father cradles his baby for the first time, the proud, beaming smile on his face vanishes only when he realises that the nappy has leaked down the inside of his sleeve.

Men who have fought in the world's bloodiest wars are apt to faint at the sight of a truly foul diaper.

Gary D. Christenson

A baby changes your dinner-party conversation from politics to poops.

Marcus Jacob Goldman, The Joy of Fatherhood

Changing a diaper is a lot like getting a present from your grandmother – you're not sure what you've got but you're pretty sure you're not going to like it.

Jeff Foxworthy

You have to change those diapers every day. When those directions on the side of the Pampers box say 'holds 6–12 pounds', they're not kidding!

Jeff Foxworthy

When it comes to changing diapers, the main thing to remember is: never scratch and sniff.

David Letterman

My baby daughter filled a diaper and there was so much poop. It didn't look like a baby's poop. It looked like a 55-year-old alcoholic took a dump.

Louis C.K.

I'm an architect for Christ sake. I build fifty-storey skyscrapers, I assemble cities of the future, I can certainly put together a goddam diaper.

Peter Mitchell, Three Men and a Baby

Spread the diaper in the position of the diamond with you at bat. Then fold second base down to home and set the baby on the pitcher's mound. Put first base and third together, bring up home plate and pin the three together. Of course, in case of rain, you gotta call the game and start all over again.

Jimmy Piersall

All babies look the same, if you ask me. I don't even know why people think they're so cute. Rolls of fat, bald, crap in their pants – just like an old man. In fact, I can guarantee that if a very old man in a nursing home walked into a room with rolls of fat, bald, and a load in his pants, not one person would go, 'Ohhh, look how cute! Can I hold him?'

Kevin Nealon, Yes, You're Pregnant, But What About Me?

I once knew a chap who had a system of just hanging the baby on the clothes line to dry and he was greatly admired by his fellow citizens for having discovered a wonderful innovation on changing a diaper.

Damon Runyon

My friend has a 16-month-old. The baby's crawling around and has an accident in his diaper. And the mother comes over and says, 'Isn't that adorable? Brandon made a gift for Daddy.' I'm thinking this guy must be real easy to shop for on Father's Day.

Garry Shandling

It's important for husbands to know when to change a diaper. I figure every three days is about right.

Alan Thicke

Some men actually enjoy changing diapers and doing late-night feedings. We must get to these men and talk sense into them before they ruin everything.

Alan Thicke

A soiled baby, with a neglected nose, cannot be conscientiously regarded as a thing of beauty.

Mark Twain

I never loved anyone so much at first meeting. But let's make no mistake why these babies come here – to replace us. We'll see who's wearing the diapers when all this is over.

Jerry Seinfeld

Babies who get colic are given something called 'gripe water'. Gripe water is 27 per cent alcohol. For babies! I was amazed, but then I thought to myself: 'Why should I be amazed – have you ever looked at babies? They're flat on their back, they can't speak and they shit themselves!'

Dave Allen

Before Kady was born, I didn't think having a kid would be such a big deal. My attitude was simple: babies are nice, play with them, put them in the closet until the next time.

Tim Allen, I'm Not Really Here

The joy of having a baby today can only be expressed in two words: tax deduction.

Anon

Q: Our baby was born last week. When will my wife start to feel normal again?
A: When the kids are in college.

Anon

Things a father should know: how to prise his wife's hands from the neck of their firstborn and clasp them round a glass of gin.

Katharine Whitehorn

A survey shows moms are better at baby talk than dads. For a dad, baby talk is: 'Here, you take him.'

Jay Leno

Ma-ma does everything for the baby, who responds by saying 'Da-da' first.

Mignon McLaughlin

Babies are equipped at birth with a number of instinctive reflexes and behaviour patterns that cause them to spend their first several years trying to kill themselves. If your home contains a sharp, toxic object, your baby will locate it; if your home contains no such object, your baby will try to obtain one via mail order.

Dave Barry

Anyone who uses the phrase 'it's as easy as taking candy from a baby' has obviously never tried taking candy from a baby.

Anon

I'm terrified of raising a kid. I can't even keep my plants alive.

Bill Maher

Don't buy one of those baby intercoms. Babies pretend to be dead. They're bastards!

Billy Connolly

I was taking on one of my father's traits… I would be looking at the stroller, asking questions about the model and how it was constructed. 'Do you like it? Any problems with it? Is it easy to fold up and put in the car? How does it handle? Are there any steering issues? Have you tried off-roading with it?'

Kevin Nealon, Yes, You're Pregnant, But What About Me?

The arrival of a baby coincides with the departure of our minds.

Bill Cosby, Fatherhood

The baby is fine; the only problem is that he looks like Edward G. Robinson.

Woody Allen

—Now, Fred. Don't say anything like you said when you saw my sister's child.

—The kid had a tail! What was I supposed to do? Pretend I didn't notice it?

Wilma and Fred Flintstone, The Flintstones

The infant was looking more than ever like some mass-assassin who has been blackballed by the Devil's Island Social and Outing Club as unfit to associate with the members.

P.G. Wodehouse, Sonny Boy

I think God made babies cute so we don't eat them.

Robin Williams

Everyone should have kids. They are the greatest joy in the world. But they are also terrorists. You'll realise as soon as they are born and they start using sleep deprivation to break you.

Ray Romano

A baby is something that gets you down in the daytime and up at night.

Anon

Bottle feeding is an opportunity for Dad to get up at 2am too.

Anon

People who say they sleep like a baby usually don't have one.

Leo J. Burke

I'm a dad now. And I'm going to do the right thing, you know. Three or four o'clock in the morning, my wife's feeding our little baby and I'm going, 'Can I help you, love?' And she says, 'Clearly not. Look at you. Curry and pies have given you many of the symptoms of the man-boob, but, as yet, the biryani does not contain that magic ingredient that will allow you to lactate. Now piss off, you're scaring the child.'

Marcus Brigstocke

—Can you take care of Emma just for today?
—Sure, just lend me your breasts and we'll be on our way.

Rachel Green and Ross Geller, Friends

Man, if I can get a burp out of that little thing I feel such a sense of accomplishment.

Brad Pitt

If you were to open up a baby's head – and I am not for a moment suggesting that you should – you would find nothing but an enormous drool gland.

Dave Barry

If you pull at babies too hard, they'll spew like a can of beer. I used to shake up my daughter, hand her to people I didn't like and say, 'Would you mind holding her a minute?'

Jeff Foxworthy

Whatever is on the floor will wind up in the baby's mouth; whatever is in the baby's mouth will wind up on the floor.

Bruce Lansky

I always wondered why babies spend so much time sucking their thumbs. Then I tasted baby food.

Robert Orben

It amazes me that a baby can be born unable to see, hear, speak, walk, or even solve the *Sun*'s coffee-time crossword, but is capable of generating a sound so loud it can dislodge masonry at forty paces.

Jeremy Clarkson

A baby is a loud noise at one end and no sense of responsibility at the other.

Ronald Knox

My friend has a baby boy. I'm recording all the noises he makes so later I can ask him what he meant.

Steven Wright

When kids hit one year old, it's like hanging out with a miniature drunk. You have to hold onto them, they bump into things, they laugh and cry, they urinate, they vomit.

Johnny Depp

Having a baby changes the way you view your in-laws. I love it when they come to visit now. They can hold the baby and I can go out.

Matthew Broderick

Dressing a baby is like putting an octopus into a string bag, making sure none of the arms hang out.

Chris Evans

At the beginning you just pray they'll have all their fingers and then later on they cause such havoc you don't even want them to have arms.

Gallagher

I used to walk into a party and scan the room for attractive women. Now I look for women to hold my baby so I can eat potato salad sitting down.

Paul Reiser

Of all the sensations of joy and release that Nature in her kindness has bestowed on the human race, there is little or nothing to beat the moment you get rid of the baby's car seat… It verges frankly on the orgasmic. As you take the wretched thing to Oxfam, you thank your stars that never again will you have to grapple with that incomprehensible buckle.

Boris Johnson

Your baby's description can be boiled down to three simple tasks – eat, sleep, and poop. You could ask him to clean out the garage, but it isn't likely to happen. Babies have an excellent union.

C.W. Nevius

I don't know why they say, 'You have a baby.' The baby has you.

Gallagher

Child's play

On a scale of difficulty, raising a child is on a par with raising the dead. If you think this is an exaggeration, try reasoning with a toddler.

The face of a child can say it all, especially the mouth part of the face.

Jack Handey

Is there any sound more terrifying on a Sunday afternoon than a child asking, 'Daddy, can we play Monopoly?'

Jeremy Clarkson

When I was a kid, my dad tried to think of ways to keep me occupied. His solution was to get my mum pregnant eight more times.

Stephen K. Amos

I tell you one thing that's great about children: they don't need a show to have fun. What do they need? A book of matches, some oily rags, a little brother… that's all they need.

Dave Attell

Living with kids is like living in a frat house… everything's broken, nobody sleeps and there's a lot of throwing up.

Ray Barone, Everybody Loves Raymond

My four-year-old twins can be charming on their own, but put them together and you've got Genghis Khan and his army in your house.

John Hannah

I wasn't really that informed about the two-year-old. Oh, I'd read about them, and occasionally I'd see documentaries on the Discovery Channel showing two-year-olds in the wild, where they belong.

Ray Romano, Everything and a Kite

From time to time children do like to share with siblings. For example, once in a while a brother will try to remove his sister's arm so he can play with it.

Bill Cosby, Fatherhood

Once when I was lost I saw a policeman and asked him to help me find my parents. I said to him: 'Do you think we'll ever find them?' He said: 'I don't know, kid. There are so many places they can hide.'

Rodney Dangerfield

I asked my father: 'How can I get my kite in the air?' He told me to run off a cliff.

Rodney Dangerfield

I could tell that my parents hated me. My bath toys were a toaster and a radio.

Rodney Dangerfield

Certain things about Hollywood used to make me angry. Now I go, 'Oh p*** off, I'm going to play Barbies with my daughter.'

Johnny Depp

I once bought my kids a set of batteries for Christmas with a note on it saying, 'Toys not included'.

Bernard Manning

Children's parties aren't the same now. What's happened to running around, bleeding, torturing the simplest member of the group – simple childhood games?

Dylan Moran

My father would take me to the playground and put me on mood swings.

Jay London

A three-year-old child is a being who gets almost as much fun out of a $300 set of swings as it does out of finding a small green caterpillar.

Bill Vaughan

The child had every toy his father wanted.

Robert C. Whitten

When I was a little kid we had a sand box. It was a quicksand box. I was an only child…eventually.

Steven Wright

Children are like pancakes – you should always throw out the first one.

Peter Benchley

There are one million obese children in Britain today. Do you realise that if they all jumped up and

down at the same time…they might lose some
bloody weight?

Jimmy Carr

When you've seen a nude infant doing a backward
somersault, you know why clothing exists.

Stephen Fry

When you let a three-year-old dress herself, she
always dresses like an East European prostitute –
pink tights, pink dress, pink shoes, little plaits and
bright red lipstick.

David Baddiel

A new father quickly learns that his child
invariably comes to the bathroom at precisely the
times when he's in there, as if he needed
company. The only way for this father to be
certain of bathroom privacy is to shave at the gas
station.

Bill Cosby

It's funny thinking that my son is probably going to be obsessed with Uncle Ewan. It'll be, 'Can Obi-Wan come over?'

Jude Law on his friend Ewan McGregor's role in Star Wars

Last Christmas my son bought me a set of monogrammed handkerchiefs with the letter 'D' on them. I said: 'Why do they have "D" on them?' He said: 'They were in the sale.'

Rick Wakeman

There's a time for being a rock star, on TV and in the studio, but you've got to put time aside for being daddy and getting chocolate rubbed in your face.

Noel Gallagher

The quickest way for a dad to get a child's attention is to sit down and look comfortable.

Lane Olinghouse

You can learn many things from children – how much patience you have, for instance.

Franklin P. Jones

Each generation has been an education for us in different ways. The first child-with-bloody-nose was rushed to an emergency room. The fifth child-with-bloody-nose was told to go to the yard immediately and stop bleeding on the carpet.

Art Linkletter

At the age of two, my son has a vocabulary of just two words but I think that girls are just born into conversation. They pop out of the womb and say, 'Are you my mother? Lovely to put a face to the name.'

Michael McIntyre

And all these children's charities like Children in Need. When was the last time you saw a child who wasn't in need and who said: 'Actually that's enough raspberry tart for me – I'm just going to clean the car'?

Dylan Moran

When you talk to a kid on the phone, you gotta remember the conversation could go in any direction. You just gotta get ready. There's no segues in the conversation. 'Dad, are you coming home tomorrow?' 'No, I'm not.' 'I have 1,000 pennies.'

Ray Romano

A two-year-old is like having a blender, but you don't have a top for it.

Jerry Seinfeld

Toddlers are crap. They're too big to pick up but too small to send to the shop for fags.

Jeff Green

Kids are great...they practically raise themselves nowadays, you know, with the Internet and all.

Homer Simpson, The Simpsons

What about the mythology we teach to young children? The Sand Man! We actually say to the young people we love: 'It's time to go to bed, because the Sand Man will come along at night and

sprinkle sand in your eyes and you'll go to sleep.'
Would *you* sleep after hearing that? Is there any
adult in the world who would sleep in a house
knowing that there's a bloody lunatic walking
around with a bag of sand? He's going to let you
have two handfuls in the eyes!

Dave Allen

Any kid will run any errand for you if you ask at
bedtime.

Red Skelton

The only thing kids use homework for is as a ploy to
stay up later when it's bedtime. They deliberately
don't tell you they've got homework, they hold it back
and then wait until you say, 'Right, switch the TV off
now, up to bed.' That's when they announce: 'I still
have homework to do – I think that trumps you, sir!'

Jack Dee

Anyone who thinks the art of conversation is dead
ought to tell a child to go to bed.

Robert C. Gallagher

When you say to a child, 'Bedtime, it's bedtime now,' that's not what the child hears. What the child hears is, 'Go and lie down in the dark...for hours... and don't move. I'm locking the door now.'

Dylan Moran

—Do you remember me having any dreams when I was a kid?

—I remember you wetting the bed.

—No, I mean, do you remember what I wanted to be.

—Dry?

Ray Barone and Frank Barone, Everybody Loves Raymond

Everyone who has ever walked barefoot into his child's room late at night hates Lego.

Tony Kornheiser

The worst sensation I know of is getting up at night and stepping on a toy train.

Kin Hubbard

Children divide into two types – the ones who come into your bed and lie still, and the ones that wriggle. Leo is a wriggler. So once he gets in, you find a foot in your ear.

Tony Blair

With kids, the days are long, but the years are short.

John Leguizamo

The terrible teens

Nothing prepares a dad for that moment when his sweet, animal-loving daughter turns overnight into a surly, rebellious monster with an attitude that would scare the average SAS squadron.

Raising teenagers is like nailing jelly to a tree.

Anon

There's nothing wrong with teenagers that reasoning with them won't aggravate.

Anon

Teenagers are incredibly well informed about any subject they don't have to study.

Anon

A teenager is always too tired to hold a dishcloth, but never too tired to hold a phone.

Anon

It's extraordinary. One day, you look at your phone bill and realise your child is a teenager.

Milton Berle

Many a man wishes he were strong enough to tear a telephone book in half – especially if he has a teenage daughter.

Guy Lombardo

It's difficult to decide whether growing pains are something teenagers have – or are.

Anon

Home is a place where teenagers go to refuel.

Anon

A babysitter is a teenager who gets two dollars an hour to eat five dollars' worth of your food.

Henny Youngman

To an adolescent, there is nothing in the world more embarrassing than a parent.

Dave Barry

I don't understand why teenage kids don't want to be seen with their parents. I was never like that. When I was at the mall with my folks and I saw my classmates, they weren't looking at me, going: 'Fugate's got a dad!'

Matt Fugate

When I was a boy of 14, my father was so ignorant I could hardly stand to have the old man around. But when I got to be 21, I was astonished at how much the old man had learned in seven years.

Mark Twain

Teenagers, are you tired of being harassed by your stupid parents? Act now. Move out, get a job, and pay your own bills – while you still know everything.

John Hinde

Your modern teenager is not about to listen to advice from an old person, defined as a person who remembers when there was no Velcro.

Dave Barry

It's amazing how quickly the kids learn to drive a car, yet are unable to understand the lawnmower, snowblower or vacuum cleaner.

Ben Bergor

—Okay, we have thirty minutes to make this house clean.
—Rub a lamp.

Dan Conner and Darlene Conner, Roseanne

I have a 16-year-old son, and 16-year-old boys have a language all of their own – a cross between Indian chief and caveman.

David Dean

Nobody understands anyone 18, including those who are 18.

Jim Bishop

I know all teenagers want a computer of their own, but if they want to lock themselves in their rooms and damage their eyesight for hours on end, they don't need a computer to do it.

Jeremy Hardy

—Your oldest daughter has been in the bathroom for, like an hour.
—An hour? What is she doing in there?
—Well, we can rule out reading.

Kerry Hennessy and Paul Hennessy, 8 Simple Rules
For Dating My Teenage Daughter

There's no need to worry about your teenagers when they're not at home. A national survey revealed that they all go to the same place – 'out' and they all do the same thing there – 'nothing'.

Bruce Lansky

Imagination is something that sits up with Dad and Mom the first time their teenager stays out late.

Lane Olinghouse

Teenagers complain there's nothing to do, then stay out all night doing it.

Bob Phillips

Now wait a second. My pretty teenage daughter with the brain of a fruit-fly earned a thousand dollars in three nights. Should I be worried?

Al Bundy, Married…with Children

Why do teenagers have six-inch steel studs embedded in the middle of their tongue? That's just one more thing for your dad to grab hold of when he's pissed off at you.

Denis Leary

My 11-year-old daughter mopes around the house all day waiting for her breasts to grow.

Bill Cosby

I got a teenage daughter and a menopausal wife. One's getting breasts, the other's getting whiskers. My life is over.

Bobby Slayton

An adolescent is a teenager who acts like a baby when you don't treat him like an adult.

Kent Crockett

Mother Nature is wonderful. She gives us 12 years to develop a love for our children before turning them into teenagers.

Eugene Bertin

Few things are more satisfying than seeing your children have teenagers of their own.

Doug Larson

The birds and the bees

One of the most important parental duties is explaining the facts of life to your child. It is a sensitive, delicate and potentially embarrassing matter, and is therefore best left to Mum.

Telling a teenager the facts of life is like giving a fish a bath.

Anon

—It turns out that Ally didn't want the sex talk! She asked me why God put us on earth.
—So what did you tell her?
—I told her heaven was too crowded.
—You what?
—And then I faked a cold and got the hell out of there.
—I don't believe this! You wanted to act like a

mature adult! Why didn't you stay and talk to her about it?

—Because I studied for the sex talk!

Ray Barone, Debra Barone, Everybody Loves Raymond

D.J. Conner: Was I an accident?

Roseanne Conner: No, D.J., you were a surprise.

D.J. Conner: Oh. What's the difference?

Roseanne Conner: Well, an accident is something that you would do over again if you had the chance. A surprise is something you didn't even know you wanted until you got it.

D.J. Conner: Oh. Was Darlene an accident?

Dan Conner: No, Darlene was a disaster.

Roseanne

—Dad, uh, can you come upstairs with me for a minute? We have to talk.

—Talk about what?

—I don't know . . . the birds and bees.

—Oh, Richard, we already had that talk.

—Yeah, and you didn't learn much.

Richie Cunningham, Howard Cunningham, Happy Days

I told my son about the birds and the bees. He told me about the butcher and my wife.

Rodney Dangerfield

They expect us to teach our kids the facts of life. I finally plucked up courage and told my son about the birds and bees. When I'd finished, I said: 'Well, son, you heard what I told you. Now what do you say?' He said: 'Not bad, Dad – you got most of it right!'

Les Dawson

Why is it the birds and the bees? It's confusing. You're 12, 13, your body's changing, hair growing in funny places, you don't know what's going on, and now Daddy tells you to filter this information through the metaphor of inter-species copulation.

Christian Finnegan

There are certain things about the human body that a 13-year-old is just not ready to process, so I believe when a man turns thirty, his dad should sit him down again and have a second 'birds and the bees' conversation, about the next chunk of his life.

'Well, son, there's going to come a time in the bee's life when maybe the stinger doesn't quite respond the way it used to...'

Christian Finnegan

I didn't know the full facts of life until I was 17. My father never talked about his work.

Martin Freud, son of Sigmund

My father made such a bad job of it. I remember something about men and women loving each other very much and then giggling something.

Hugh Grant

My father told me all about the birds and the bees, the liar. I went steady with a woodpecker till I was 21.

Bob Hope

You know your children are growing up when they stop asking you where they came from and refuse to tell you where they're going.

P.J. O'Rourke

When my father was trying to tell me about sex, a lecture that involved birds' nests and sparrows' eggs, I asked him what kind of sex education he had received. He said the local vicar, who was also the captain of his first cricket team, had warned him that inappropriate touching of his willy would make it fall off.

Michael Parkinson, Parky: My Autobiography

Dad said he would give me a £5 note if I got a barmaid pregnant.

John Peel

The sexual briefing that I got from my father was memorable for the way it avoided textbook jargon and came directly to the point. He told me I was never to use a men's room in the Broadway subway. This dissertation left a certain gap in the story of procreation.

Ralph Schoenstein

I was told that you could get pregnant by sitting in a married man's bath water, so I always gave the bath a good rinse if my father had been in before me.

Julie Walters, That's Another Story

Talking to kids is hard. My son asked me, 'Dad, where do babies come from?' I said, 'You know, son, my dad never told me, but I'm gonna tell you straight up. Mummy bends over like this. Here, just watch the tape. You're on it. Sort of. Good swimmer. Proud of you, boy.'

Basil White

The dating game

A dad's views on his children dating are governed solely by their sex. Sons are encouraged to go out and play the field, daughters are encouraged to stay in and play the piano.

I hope she (my daughter Dakota) doesn't end up with the kind of scallywag I was at twenty! I'm always teasing, 'I'll put my Zorro suit on and that will teach him.'

Antonio Banderas

You worry about your daughter meeting the wrong kind of guy… Then you stop worrying about her meeting the wrong guy, and you worry about her meeting the right guy. That's the greatest fear of all, because then you lose her.

George Banks, Father of the Bride

Well, he's better than that Stuart lad you went out with from the flats…he was a gormless git him, he couldn't find his arse with both hands.

Jim Royle, The Royle Family

I will show him the same kind of respect that any father would show a 41-year-old man who dates his teenage daughter.

Al Bundy, Married…with Children

Watching your daughter being collected by her date feels like handing over a million-dollar Stradivarius to a gorilla.

Jim Bishop

Any astronomer can predict with absolute accuracy just where every star in the universe will be at 11.30 tonight. He can make no such prediction about his teenage daughter.

James T. Adams

And I'll get to sleep at night – the deep slumber of a father whose daughters aren't out being impregnated.

Walter Stratford, 10 Things I Hate About You

—Do you know what time it is?
—A watch doesn't really go with this outfit, Daddy.

Mel Horowitz, Cher Horowitz, Clueless

Someone told me that if you get your daughter into ponies, it delays her interest in boys for five years. Emily has five ponies, so we are sorted!

Martin Clunes

A father knows exactly what those boys at the mall have in their depraved little minds because he once owned such a depraved little mind himself. In fact, if he thinks enough about the plans that he used to have for young girls, the father not only will support his wife in keeping their daughter home but he might even run over to the mall and have a few of those boys arrested.

Bill Cosby

My daughter's online with her friends, and little boys are starting to call the house. We had a kid call the house at two in the morning. Oh, I lost it. 'Cause first of all, I'm off in la-la land with Shania Twain in the mountains somewhere. I hear a phone ring and I'm like, 'Who's got a phone in the mountains?' So when I realise it's my phone, I'm already a little miffed, so I go, 'Hello!' And this little voice says, 'Uh…is Emily there?' And I go, 'Dude, if you have a brain in your skull, you will hang this phone up right now!' Click. Then my wife turns to me and goes, 'Bill, you've got to be nice.' And I go, 'No, ma'am, "nice" stops at midnight!'

Bill Engvall

—Oh come on, Dad. Do you really think that in
six months I will be more prepared to date?
—No, but I will.

Kerry Hennessy, Paul Hennessy, 8 Simple Rules For
Dating My Teenage Daughter

You have other girlfriends, Kyle, and that's fine with
me – as long as it's okay with my daughter.
Otherwise, you will continue to date her and no
one but her, until she is finished with you. Because
if you make her cry, I will make you cry.

Paul Hennessy, 8 Simple Rules For Dating My Teenage
Daughter

If they bring a group of guys over to the house to
have a pool party or whatever, I just say, 'Dude,
what's your name?' and he says, 'Uh, Cinjun.' Then
I say, 'Okay, Cinjun, you're in charge. If anything
happens to one of my daughters, I'm coming to you
first, and then I'm going to kill all your friends right
in front of you. And you'll be last.'

Bruce Willis

My eldest daughter brought a boy home the other day and I reacted quite badly. She came in and said: 'Alright Dad, this is Billy.' She went out of the room and I went up to this Billy and said: 'If you so much as touch her, I'll cut you!' This Billy starts crying. Still that's seven-year-olds for you.

Phill Jupitus

—You know how I want your sisters to date only the good guys? Well, I want you to be a good guy.
—You want me to date my sisters?

Paul Hennessy, Rory Hennessy, 8 Simple Rules For
Dating My Teenage Daughter

What's with you, kid? You think the death of Sammy Davis left an opening in the Rat Pack?

Mel Horowitz, Clueless

The girl doesn't understand that the boy is 15 years old. At 15, the boy would hit on a snake.

Cliff Huxtable, The Cosby Show

When your daughter's date shows up, casually show him your collection of five shrunken heads, then yell up to your daughter, 'Honey, Number Six is here!'

David Letterman

If you think there are no new frontiers, watch a boy ring the front doorbell on his first date.

Olin Miller

I've got seven kids. The three words you hear most around my house are: 'Hello,' 'Goodbye,' and 'I'm pregnant.'

Dean Martin

What is a dad?

A dad is basically a simple creature who just wants his children to be happy with a good education, a well-paid job and a solid relationship – as long as none of this interferes with him watching sport on TV.

A father is someone who carries pictures where his money used to be.

Anon

Father is the guy who's quick to appear with the camera and just as quick to disappear when there's a diaper to be changed.

Joan Rivers

Fatherhood is pretending the present you love most is soap-on-a-rope.

Bill Cosby

Fatherhood is telling your daughter that Michael Jackson loves all his fans, but has special feelings for the ones who eat broccoli.

Bill Cosby

The place of the father in the modern suburban family is a very small one, particularly if he plays golf.

Bertrand Russell

Fathers are biological necessities, but social accidents.

Margaret Mead

You know you're a dad when the sentence, 'Darling, could you take his foot out of my pocket?' sounds normal.

Anon

You know you're a dad when the list of bodily fluids that disgust you has shortened to zero.

Anon

You know you're a dad when you're used to doing everything one-handed.

Anon

You know you're a dad when you discover that not only have you developed an opinion about crib bumpers, but you have actually uttered it aloud.

Steve Johnson

You know you're a dad when at birthday parties you start assessing which little boy or girl seems like a good catch for your pride and joy. That you are doing this based on their ability to stack blocks fails to strike you as ridiculous.

Steve Johnson

You know you're a dad when for the first time in your life, the vomit you are covered in is not of your own making.

Steve Johnson

You know you're a dad when you spend 45 minutes sweating and grunting in the backseat of a car. You are alone; when you are finished, the car seat is installed.

Steve Johnson

A woman knows all about her children. She knows about dental appointments and football games and romances and best friends and favourite foods and secret fears and hopes and dreams. A man is vaguely aware of some short people living in the house.

Dave Barry

When I was a little kid, a father was like the light in the refrigerator: every house had one, but no one really knew what either of them did once the door was shut.

Erma Bombeck

It's not easy to juggle a pregnant wife and a troubled child, but somehow I managed to fit in eight hours of TV a day.

Homer Simpson, The Simpsons

When you're a parent, you give up your freedom. You sleep according to someone else's schedule, you eat according to someone else's schedule. It's like being in jail, but you really love the warden.

Lew Schneider

What makes a man a man is not the ability to have a child but to raise one.

Barack Obama

Bank of Dad

From children's toys to teenage loans and eventually a wedding to grace the pages of Hello! *magazine, Dad is viewed by his children as a non-stop source of income. He might not be the bank that likes to say 'yes' but he is often too soft a touch to say 'no'.*

When your children get to be teenagers, they think that they can con you with money. And they do. 'Can I borrow a fiver?' 'Yeah.' Two weeks later: 'Can I borrow a tenner?' 'But you owe me a fiver.' 'Well, give me the tenner, and I'll give you a fiver.' Two weeks later: 'Can I have a twenty?' 'But you owe me a tenner.' 'Well, give me a twenty and I'll give you back ten.' It goes on to the point where my son will say to me: 'Can I have a hundred quid?' I'll say: 'No, you can't. I'm sick and tired of lending you money!' And he'll say to me: 'I always pay you back, don't I?'

Dave Allen

A father is a cash-point machine in trousers.

Anon

You can always rely on dad cabs: 24-hour service and no meter.

Anon

Mother Nature, in her infinite wisdom, has instilled within each of us a powerful biological instinct to reproduce; this is her way of assuring that the human race, come what may, will never have any disposable income.

Dave Barry

I believe that we parents must encourage our children to become educated, so they can get into a good college that we cannot afford.

Dave Barry

If you want to recapture your youth, just cut off his allowance.

Al Bernstein

I wish to thank my parents for making this night possible…and my children for making it necessary.

Victor Borge

Money: the one thing that keeps us in touch with our children.

Gyles Brandreth

Children really brighten up a household – they never turn the lights off.

Ralph Bus

You know why John D. Rockefeller had all that money? Because he had only one child, so he didn't have to spend $90,000 on Snoopy pens and Superhero mugs and Smurf pyjamas and Barbie Ferraris.

Bill Cosby, Fatherhood

Boy, you and Niles! It's been the same since you were kids. If one of you has something, the other one always has to have it, too. I had to buy two Balinese lutes, two decoupage kits, two pairs of lederhosen. When you finally moved out of the house, that was one embarrassing garage sale.

Martin Crane, Frasier

There are times when parenthood seems nothing but feeding the mouth that bites you.

Peter De Vries, The Tunnel of Love

If a man smiles in his own house, someone is sure to ask him for money.

William Feather

A father is a banker provided by nature.

French proverb

My daughter wanted a new pair of trainers. I told her, 'You're 11, make your own.'

Jeremy Hardy

Years ago I asked my dad for a boob job but he said it would cheapen my image.

Paris Hilton

Husbands are a small band of men, armed only with wallets, besieged by a horde of wives and children.

P.J. O'Rourke

When one of Lisa's baby teeth fell out here, the tooth fairy left her 50 cents. Another tooth fell out when she was with her father in Las Vegas, and that tooth fairy left her $5. When I told Elvis that 50 cents would be more in line, he laughed. He knew I was not criticising him; how would Elvis Presley know the going rate for a tooth?

Priscilla Presley

—Dad, where were you when Kennedy was killed?
—What? Kennedy's dead?

—Well, you know they say everybody remembers where they were when they heard he was killed?

—Well, I don't remember, but I bet our bloody immersion heater was on!

Antony Royle, Jim Royle, The Royle Family

I can always count on getting one thing for Father's Day – all the bills from Mother's Day.

Milton Berle

Father's Day is the day when father goes broke giving his family money so they can surprise him with gifts he doesn't need.

Richard Taylor

A truly rich man is one whose children run into his arms when his hands are empty.

Anon

I remember sex

An addition to the family means that sex often has to take a back seat…which ironically may be where conception occurred. Not only are women tired during pregnancy -- and for the first twenty years after childbirth -- but they really don't want to be reminded of what put them in that state in the first place.

A father is a man who prefers sleep over sex.

Ralph Anderson

—You're sure it's safe for the baby if we have sex while you're pregnant?
—No offence, but I don't think you're going to reach.

Adam Williams, Rachel Bradley, Cold Feet

My dad's become obsessed by dogging since he read about it in the *Mail on Sunday*. He'll be driving along and say, 'Look at that dogging,' and I say, 'No, Dad, it's a car boot sale.'

Alan Carr

Children always assume the sexual lives of their parents come to a grinding halt at their conception.

Alan Bennett

My mum told me the best time to ask my dad for anything was during sex. Not the best advice I've ever been given. I burst in through the bedroom door saying, 'Can I have a new bike?' He was very upset. His secretary was surprisingly nice about it. I got the bike.

Jimmy Carr

When my old man wanted sex, my mother would show him a picture of me.

Rodney Dangerfield

I've learned that as a parent, when you have sex, your body emits a hormone that drifts down the hall into your child's room and makes them want a drink of water.

Jeff Foxworthy

Kids. They're not easy. But there has to be some penalty for sex.

Bill Maher

After kids, everything changes. We're having sex about every three months. If I have sex, I know my quarterly estimated taxes are due. And if it's oral sex, I know it's time to renew my driver's licence.

Ray Romano

My father was quite a naughty lad in his time. Daddy did his bit for heterosexuality, as I have tried to do mine.

Joan Collins

—Lois, you've got a sick mind.

—Peter, I'm talking about making love.

—Oh, I thought you wanted us to murder the children and harvest their organs for beer money.

Peter Griffin, Lois Griffin, Family Guy

When you wake up one day and say, 'You know what? I don't think I ever need to sleep or have sex again.' Congratulations, you're ready to have children.

Ray Romano, Everything and a Kite

—Tim, do you ever listen to me? It was the last thing I said in bed to you last night.

—No, I believe, if you recall, the last thing you said to me in bed last night was 'NO!'

Jill Taylor, Tim Taylor, Home Improvement

Embarrassing Dad

Whether it's dancing at weddings like a man trapped in a threshing machine, calling their young son by his pet name in front of his school friends or doing impressions of Frank Spencer in crowded restaurants, dads have a built-in capacity for embarrassing their offspring.

And when I'm drunk, I dance like me dad.

Robbie Williams, 'Strong'

I told my son that if he turns into a moody teenager, I'm not going to yell at him, I'm not going to ground him, I'm just going to show up at school… wearing moon boots, Hammer pants, Frankie Says Relax T-shirt, three-and-a-half-foot sombrero…

Matt Fugate

I know when I grow up my kids will be embarrassed of me. Because no matter how cool your parents are, you're always gonna be embarrassed of them. Do you think Jesus was embarrassed of his dad? He'd be like, 'Yeah, my dad created the world, but he's not THAT cool.' Or, 'It's fine, Dad, just drop me here in this manger… Yeah, he's picking me up sometime around Easter.'

Jim Gaffigan

One time my father caught me watching a porno movie. The one thing you never want to hear in that situation is, 'Son, move over.'

Dave Attell

Watching sex on telly with your parents – that's embarrassing. I didn't even know they knew how to use the camcorder.

Jimmy Carr

—Drive carefully. And don't forget to fasten your condom.

—Dad!

—Seat belt! I meant, I meant seat belt.

George Banks, Annie Banks, Father of the Bride

Well, I'd like to say a nice big thank you to Emma for putting to one side all our doubts about our Antony being a sausage jockey.

Jim Royle, The Royle Family

Fathers are more fun than mothers because fathers are the only people in the house who are allowed to have gas.

Bill Cosby

I think it's ironic that for once Dad's butt prevented the release of toxic gas.

Bart Simpson, The Simpsons

My dad won't say, 'Close the door.' Instead he says, 'The door's not an arsehole – it won't shut by itself!'

Steve Patterson

—Would somebody like to listen to my
announcement?
—Switched at birth. Please say I was switched at
birth.

Paul Hennessy, Kerry Hennessy, 8 Simple Rules For
Dating My Teenage Daughter

Don't bring home one of these young ones, Dad –
no one younger than me, please.

Jade Jagger

Other people and their English social rituals
frightened my father. Once at a wedding, a
dreaded occasion, he advanced towards the
greeting party and kissed the bride's father by
mistake.

Griff Rhys Jones, Semi-Detached

The most embarrassing thing you can do as a
schoolchild is to call your teacher 'Mum' or 'Dad'.

Peter Kay

I watched the Will Smith movie *The Pursuit of Happyness* with my three sons, and at the end I observed solemnly, 'The motto of this film is always live your dreams, boys – then you can achieve anything.' There was a contemplative silence, until Stanley, 11, finally responded, very slowly, on behalf of the group: 'Oh, God! Dad thinks he's Martin Luther King.'

Piers Morgan

Getting down on all fours and imitating a rhinoceros stops babies from crying. I don't know why parents don't do this more often. Usually it makes the kid laugh. Sometimes it sends him into shock. Either way it quiets him down. If you're a parent, acting like a rhino has another advantage. Keep it up until the kid is a teenager and he definitely won't have his friends hanging around your house all the time.

P.J. O'Rourke

My dad still has this knack of embarrassing me. I have this dream that I'm at Buckingham Palace collecting my MBE from the Queen for being a smashing guy and he says: 'Do you know he didn't have a proper girlfriend till he was 19?'

Gary Strang, Men Behaving Badly

I suppose that the high-water mark of my youth in Columbus, Ohio, was the night the bed fell on my father.

James Thurber

I'm Dad. I do what I want to do! I walk around buck naked. My kids hate it, but I walk around the house with no drawers on.

Tracy Morgan

—I have decided to put an end to this madness that is ruining all our lives.

—You're going to kill Dad?

Susan Harper, Michael Harper, My Family

A job for life

If you think your duties are over once the toys have been put away in the loft, you're wrong. With regard to your house, it is easier to remove rising damp than the average twenty-something son.

The American Dream is not to own your own home but to get your kids out of it.

Dick Armey

My mother wanted me to go to Ohio State. My father just wanted me to go.

Bob Hope

Parenting never ends. It's like your Aunt Edna's ass. It goes on forever and it's just as frightening.

Frank Buckman, Parenthood

Parenthood is a lot easier to get into than out of.

Bruce Lansky

Becoming a father is easy enough, but being one can be very rough.

Wilhelm Busch

I won't lie to you, fatherhood isn't easy like motherhood.

Homer Simpson, The Simpsons

A man's children and his garden both reflect the amount of weeding done during the growing season.

Anon

My father used to play with my brother and me in the yard. Mother would come out and say, 'You're tearing up the grass.' 'We're not raising grass,' Dad would reply. 'We're raising boys.'

Harmon Killebrew

There isn't a child who hasn't gone out into the brave new world who doesn't eventually return to the old homestead carrying a bundle of dirty clothes.

Art Buchwald

Moving back in with your parents is like getting busted on a parole violation and being thrown back in the slammer.

Jerry Seinfeld

This is the hardest truth for a father to learn: that his children are continuously growing up and moving away from him – until, of course, they move back in.

Bill Cosby

Human beings are the only creatures on earth that allow their children to come back home.

Bill Cosby

Learning to dislike children at an early age saves a lot of expense and aggravation later in life.

Robert Byrne

My childhood should have taught me lessons for my own parenthood, but it didn't because parenting can be learned only by people who have no children.

Bill Cosby

Setting a good example for children takes all the fun out of middle age.

William Feather

I cannot think of any need in childhood as strong as the need for a father's protection.

Sigmund Freud

One father is more than a hundred schoolmasters.

George Herbert

Like any father, I have moments when I wonder whether I belong to the children or they belong to me.

Bob Hope

What a father says to his children is not heard by the world but it will be heard by posterity.

Jean Paul Richter

Fatherhood, for me, has been less a job than an unstable and surprising combination of adventure, blindman's buff, guerrilla warfare and crossword puzzle.

Frederic F. Van De Water

Head of the house

Everyone knows it's Dad who is head of the house, traditionally the breadwinner, the one whose word is final. Mum just makes all the decisions.

My dad thinks he wears the trousers in our house, but it's always Mum who tells him which pair to put on.

Anon

My dad wore the trousers in our family – at least, after the court order.

Anon

—Alright Ally, you have to do what Mommy says.

—Why?

—'Cos I do.

Ray Barone, Ally Barone, Everybody Loves Raymond

I am not the boss of my house. I don't know when I lost it. I don't know if I ever had it. But I have seen the boss's job and I do not want it.

Bill Cosby

Today, while the titular head of the family may still be the father, everyone knows that he is little more than chairman, at most, of the entertainment committee.

Ashley Montagu

(*Meeting aliens*) Please don't eat me! I have a wife and kids. Eat them!

Homer Simpson, The Simpsons

—My dad was a nun.

—No he wasn't, Baldrick.

—He was too, sir. 'Cause whenever he was up in court and the judge asked 'occupation', he'd say 'none'.

Private Baldrick, Captain Blackadder, Blackadder Goes Forth

My father played the viola in the Royal Danish Symphony Orchestra. A lot of people don't know the difference between a violin and a viola. Unfortunately, my father was one of them.

Victor Borge

My father was stupid. He worked in a bank and they caught him stealing pens.

Rodney Dangerfield

My father was in the horse artillery, but the feed bag kept falling off his ears.

Les Dawson

I don't have a movie that my kids can see. So up until tonight, they knew mommy is an actress and daddy makes pancakes. So thank you. Now they know what their father does.

Michael Douglas, accepting a Hollywood Lifetime Achievement award

My dad was a roofer, so Dad if you're up there…

Stewart Francis

I remember the shouts of 'Scab!' as my father went to work. 'Scab!' they would shout during the great dermatologists' strike.

Harry Hill

When my daughter was about seven years old, she asked me one day what I did at work. I told her I worked at the college – that my job was to teach people how to draw. She stared at me, incredulous, and said, 'You mean they forget?'

Howard Ikemoto

Every time I'm about ready to go to bed with a guy, I have to look at my dad's name all over his underwear.

Marci Klein, daughter of Calvin Klein

Son, if you really want something in this life, you have to work for it. Now quiet! They're about to announce the lottery numbers.

Homer Simpson, The Simpsons

The girls have very high status in my house. I'm the git in the family.

Clive Owen

A chip off the old block

Children often seek to emulate their fathers, but whereas some dads act as a shining example, others serve more as a warning.

He followed in his father's footsteps, but his gait was somewhat erratic.

Nicolas Bentley

Maybe the best thing we can do is to make sure that our children are a slight improvement on us.

Sanjeev Bhaskar

If I turn into my parents, I'll either be an alcoholic blond chasing after twenty-year-old boys or…I'll end up like my mom.

Chandler Bing, Friends

My dad said, 'Alan, why are you doing this to me?' I said, 'I don't know, Dad, but I can show you through expressive dance.'

> *Alan Carr, telling his football manager dad*
> *Graham that he was going to study performing arts*
> *rather than follow in his sporting footsteps*

I am often asked if it is because of some genetic trait that I stand with my hands behind me, like my father. The answer is that we both have the same tailor. He makes our sleeves so tight that we can't get our hands in front.

> *Prince Charles*

I always looked up to my father, but then again I look up to everyone.

> *Ronnie Corbett*

My father didn't want anyone following in his footsteps: he was a burglar.

> *Les Dawson*

I grew up to have my father's looks, my father's speech patterns, my father's posture, my father's walk, my father's opinions, and my mother's contempt for my father.

Jules Feiffer

I am an expert on electricity. My father occupied the chair of applied electricity at the state prison.

W.C. Fields

I could never figure out why my father was always in the garage. Then I got married and it became crystal clear.

Billy Gardell

—I mean, you're a doctor and Mom's a lawyer, but I don't love you any less, because you're my dad. So instead of being disappointed that I'm not like you, maybe you should be happy and love me anyway, because I'm your son.

—Theo, that's the dumbest thing I've ever heard! No wonder you get Ds in everything. You're afraid to try because you're afraid your brain is going to explode and it's going to ooze out of your ear. Now you are going to try because I said so. I am your father. I brought you into this world and I will take you out.

Theo Huxtable, Cliff Huxtable, The Cosby Show

My father had a profound influence on me, he was a lunatic.

Spike Milligan

I want to die like my father, peacefully in his sleep. Not screaming and terrified, like his passengers.

Bob Monkhouse

A man's desire for a son is usually nothing but the wish to duplicate himself in order that such a remarkable pattern may not be lost to the world.

Helen Rowland

The fundamental defect of fathers is that they want their children to be a credit to them.

Bertrand Russell

—You don't have to follow in my footsteps, son.
—Don't worry – I don't even like using the
bathroom after you.

Homer Simpson, Bart Simpson, The Simpsons

—I am through with working. Working is for
chumps.
—Son, I'm proud of you! I was twice your age when
I figured that out.

Bart Simpson, Homer Simpson, The Simpsons

—You must come and visit us when we move in.
—Yes, I heard you blew Hilda's cottage up.
—Now, actually, that wasn't me, it was my dad.
—So that's where you get it from.

Howard Steel, Yvonne Cook, The Worst Week of My Life

I've got my dad's eyes, knock-knees, ugly feet and
big nose.

Rod Stewart

My father wanted to know every detail about the baby. I said she took after him. Half bald and angry-looking.

Sue Townsend, The Growing Pains of Adrian Mole

He's strong, he's smart, he's tough, he's vicious, he's violent – all the ingredients you need to be an entrepreneur.

Donald Trump, on ten-month-old son Baron

When my son was born, I had this dream that one day he might grow up to be a Nobel Prize winner. But I also had another dream that he might grow up to say, 'Do you want fries with that?'

Robin Williams

My father was a very silly man. And it has always been a philosophy of mine that nothing is so painful in life that it can't be laughed at, and that is something I learnt from him.

Mike Myers

Who'd be a dad?

Kids: when they're not a drain on your wallet, they're a drain on your emotions. So there are days when every dad must wonder whether simply renting a child for a few weeks would not have been a better option. After all, it's a method that seems to work okay with DVDs.

Debra Barone: Honey, show Daddy what you drew.
Ray Barone: Um, let's see. A big wall of red?
Ally Barone: No.
Debra Barone: Ally told me that was a picture of you in hell.

Everybody Loves Raymond

I've noticed that one thing about parents is that no matter what stage your child is at, the parents who have older children always tell you the next stage is worse.

Dave Barry

Being a father is like doing drugs – you smell bad, get no sleep and spend all your money on them.

Paul Bettany

If the new American father feels bewildered and even defeated, let him take comfort from the fact that whatever he does in any fathering situation has a fifty per cent chance of being right.

Bill Cosby

By the time the youngest children have learned to keep the house tidy, the oldest grandchildren are on hand to tear it to pieces.

Christopher Morley

I have just returned from a children's party. I'm one of the survivors.

Percy French

Hosting your children's party is like an exercise in riot control. You find yourself spotting the ringleaders, appealing to the more moderate children to try and keep order, abandoning the living room to the mob, and trying to consolidate your power base in the kitchen.

Jeremy Hardy

Having one child makes you a parent; having two you are a referee.

David Frost

Parents are not interested in justice, they're interested in peace and quiet.

Bill Cosby

—That's my brother, Niles. He's a little…how would you describe Niles, Dad?
—I usually just change the subject.

Frasier Crane, Martin Crane, Frasier

With my 12-year-old daughter emotions are running high. Anything can set her off – simple things like, 'Do you want more carrots?' 'What does that mean?! I hate you, I'm going to my room!'

David Dean

Forget about surviving forty years in the music business. Just surviving 27 years of Nicole Richie has been a struggle-and-a-half, I want to tell you. I stand here as a survivor, I want you to know, for all the parents out there.

Lionel Richie

People treat children as though there is something wrong with them because they're ignorant and small. They say, 'I'm so worried about Alexander's development. I mean, he's got no grasp of bonded numbers, no concept of phonics, his hand-to-eye co-ordination is all over the place. I mean, goodness knows what he's going to be like when he's born.'

Jeremy Hardy, Grumpy Old Men

Kids are wonderful, but I like mine barbecued.

Bob Hope

I forgot, some of the greatest lies ever told by your children: 'I'll pay you back later.' 'It was like that when I found it.'

Cliff Huxtable, The Cosby Show

Children are unpredictable. You never know what inconsistency they're going to catch you in next.

Franklin P. Jones

The last family pet that we ever had was a dog called Oscar. He was a cross between a springer spaniel and a little bastard. Well, that's what my dad used to shout whenever he came downstairs and slipped at the bottom in Oscar's shit.

Peter Kay, The Sound of Laughter

Signs that your kids hate you:
- When they need batteries, they always seem to take ones from the smoke detector above your bed.
- Their Father's Day gift: for one day, they don't call you 'lardass'.
- They keep leaving phone numbers of divorce lawyers in Mum's purse.

- Their pet goldfish are called We, Hate and Dad.
- Your oldest boy has a bumper sticker which reads: 'I'd rather be at my father's funeral.'
- They say to Mum: 'Is he really the best you could do?'
- They hold a tribal council and vote you out of the family.

David Letterman

My kids hate me. Every Father's Day they give a 'World's Greatest Dad' mug to the milkman.

Rodney Dangerfield

—I don't say this often enough, but, uh, I'm gonna die…

—High five, anyone?

Peter Griffin, Stewie Griffin, Family Guy

What are children anyway? Midget drunks. They greet you in the morning by kneeing you in the face and talking gibberish. They can't even walk straight.

Dylan Moran

Having a family is like having a bowling alley installed in your brain.

Martin Mull

When I am trying to manage the kids at Christmas I can understand why some animals eat their young.

Brendan O'Carroll

Insanity is hereditary. You can get it from your children.

Sam Levenson

The one thing children wear out faster than shoes is parents.

John J. Plomp

Parents like the idea of kids, they just don't like *their* kids.

Morley Safer

When I look at the smiles on all the children's faces, I just know they're about to jab me with something.

Homer Simpson, The Simpsons

—Why does bad stuff always happen to me?

—Hey, don't worry. Bad stuff happens to me all the time.

—Yeah, but you cause it.

Randy Taylor, Tim Taylor, Home Improvement

Before I was married, I had a hundred theories about raising children and no children. Now I have three children and no theories.

John Wilmot

My son is 21. He'll be 22 if I let him.

Henny Youngman

The first half of our lives is ruined by our parents, and the second half by our children.

Clarence Darrow

When I was a boy I used to do what my father wanted. Now I have to do what my boy wants. My problem is, when am I going to do what I want?

Sam Levenson

Children are a great comfort in your old age – and they help you reach it faster, too.

Lionel Kauffman

Fatherly advice

Dads are only too willing to dispense advice to their children in the form of pearls of wisdom accumulated from years of experience. The problem is finding someone who'll listen.

The best time to give advice to your children is while they're still young enough to believe you know what you're talking about.

Anon

Every father should remember that one day his son will follow his example instead of his advice.

Anon

My father used to say, 'Never accept a drink from a urologist.'

Erma Bombeck

My father always used to say, 'What doesn't kill you, makes you stronger' … till the accident.

Jimmy Carr

When I was at school, I was perpetually punched in the head by other kids. So my dad sent me off to learn boxing … where I was perpetually punched in the head by other kids.

Lee Evans

My father told me that if I ever met a lady in a dress like yours, I must look her straight in the eyes.

Prince Charles to actress Susan Hampshire who was wearing an extremely low-cut dress

My dad always used to tell me that if they challenge you to an after-school fight, tell them you won't wait – you can kick their ass right now.

Cameron Diaz

My dad said: 'Always be a moving target, son, because a moving target is very difficult to hit.'

Lee Evans

Pictures speak louder than words. Because some words are big and hard to understand.

Peter Griffin, Family Guy

My dad used to say, 'Always fight fire with fire,' which is probably why he got thrown out of the fire brigade.

Harry Hill

He didn't tell me how to live; he lived, and let me watch him do it.

Clarence Budington Kelland

Likely as not, the child you can do the least with will do the most to make you proud.

Mignon McLaughlin

In our family, the rule was: never keep a soda can between your legs when you're in the car. My father told us this wicked story about a man who was driving with a can between his legs and got into a bad car wreck. And bang, he lost his Johnson! To this day, I cannot drive with a can between my legs.

Brad Pitt

My father had always said there are four things a child needs: plenty of love, nourishing food, regular sleep, and lots of soap and water. After that, what he needs most is some intelligent neglect.

Ivy Baker Priest

I have always had the feeling I could do anything and my dad told me I could. I was in college before I found out he might be wrong.

Ann Richards

My dad used to say: 'Keep your chin up, son.' He once broke his jaw walking into a lamppost.

Adam Sandler

My dad said: 'Marry a girl with the same beliefs as the family.' I thought: 'Dad, why should I marry a girl who thinks I'm a schmuck?'

Adam Sandler

Kids, you tried your best and you failed miserably. The lesson is, never try.

Homer Simpson, The Simpsons

My father put me on a table and said: 'Jump and I'll catch you.' I jumped and he took his hands away and I fell on the floor. He picked me up and stroked my hair and said: 'Never trust anybody in your life. Not even your own father.'

Freddie Starr

My father said, 'The less you say in a relationship, the less you can be wrong.'

Joe Starr

My dad's solution to every injury was, 'Walk it off.' 'Bloody nose? Walk it off! Diarrhoea? Walk it off!'

Bob Stromberg

I'm glad I was raised by my dad. There are things you can learn from a father, as a son, that you can never learn from Mom. Special things, important things, like 'Never challenge Dad to a fist fight.'

Christopher Titus

I have found out that the best way to give advice to your children is to find out what they want and then advise them to do it.

Harry S. Truman

When I was ten, my pa told me never to talk to strangers. We haven't spoken since.

Steven Wright

I asked my old man if I could go ice-skating on the lake. He told me, 'Wait till it gets warmer.'

Rodney Dangerfield

My son complains about headaches. I tell him all the time, 'When you get out of bed, it's feet first!'

Henny Youngman

My father used to say: 'Better to keep your mouth shut and be thought a fool than to open it and leave no doubt.'

Carol Thatcher

Family outings

Five minutes after setting off from home in the car, your child asks: 'Are we there yet?' Two minutes later, he announces: 'I want to be sick.' Welcome to the family outing...

Travel sickness blighted our every car journey. One out of the three of us was sick every time Dad drove more than 500 yards.

Andrew Collins, Where Did It All Go Right?

Martin Crane: Remember the old days, Niles? When they were kids, all they had in the back seat was a mayonnaise jar!

Frasier Crane: Yes, it took quite a bit of skill to use it
    successfully at 70mph! Never really been fond of
    mayonnaise since.
Niles Crane: Or speed bumps.

Frasier

Those were awful, those family driving vacations.
Dad insisting on covering as many miles as possible
in a day; the two of us, tiny hostages in the back
seat, clutching our car sickness bags, straining to
see something out of the window as the landscape
whizzed by. I was 13 before I realised cows aren't
blurry.

Niles Crane, Frasier

Every year my family would pile into the car for our
vacation and drive 80 trillion miles just to prove we
couldn't get along in any setting.

Janeane Garofalo

The memories of my family outings are still a
source of strength to me. I remember we'd all pile
into the car – I forget what kind it was – and drive

and drive. I'm not sure where we'd go, but I think there were some trees there. The smell of something was strong in the air as we played whatever sport we played. I remember a bigger, older guy we called 'Dad'. We'd eat some stuff, or not, and then I think we went home. I guess some things never leave you.

Jack Handey

If you ever want to torture my dad, tie him up and right in front of him, refold a road map incorrectly.

Cathy Ladman

'Are you lost, Daddy?' I asked tenderly. 'Shut up,' he explained.

Ring Lardner

What Dad means by 'see' of course is 'drive past at 67 miles per hour'. Dad feels it is a foolish waste of valuable vacation time to get out of the car and actually go look at an attraction.

Dave Barry

I'm addicted to cars – I'm thinking of checking into the Henry Ford Clinic.

Tim Taylor, Home Improvement

We have not even got to the car, and already Alistair has called Tim a 'stupid bloody prat' and Tim has called Alistair an 'idiotic git'. Nine-thirty in the morning and already the air is turning sulphurous.

Charles Jennings, Fathers' Race

When I'd fight with my sister in the back seat of the car, my dad would say: 'Right, that's it. Do you want me to come back there?' I thought that was a fascinating idea … since he was driving.

Bob Stromberg

If you ever start feeling like you have the goofiest, craziest, most dysfunctional family in the world, all you have to do is go to a state fair. Because five minutes at the fair, you'll be going, 'You know, we're alright. We are dang near royalty.'

Jeff Foxworthy

You know you're getting old when you start to like your mum and dad again. 'Yes, I'd love to come caravanning to Tenby with you. No, I'll bring a packed lunch. I'm not paying café prices.'

Jeff Green

In America there are two classes of travel – first class and with children.

Robert Benchley

My parents used to take me to the pet department and tell me it was a zoo.

Billy Connolly

A petting zoo is a great place if you want your kid's clothes to end up inside a goat's stomach.

Bill Dwyer

When I was a kid, I said to my father one afternoon, 'Daddy, will you take me to the zoo?' He answered, 'If the zoo wants you, let them come and get you.'

Jerry Lewis

I don't know how much my parents loved me as a kid. They took me to the safari park to see the lions… in an antelope skinned jacket… with a roast chicken in each pocket.

John Moloney

Sorry, Meg, no trip to the mall today. Daddy loves ya, but Daddy also loves *Star Trek*, and in all fairness, *Star Trek* was here first.

Peter Griffin, Family Guy

It is admirable for a man to take his son fishing, but there is a special place in heaven for the father who takes his daughter shopping.

John Sinor

Hot dogs always seem better out than at home; so do French fried potatoes; so do your children.

Mignon McLaughlin

Babies don't need a vacation, but I still see them at the beach. I'll go over to them and say, 'What are you doing here? You've never worked a day in your life!'

Steven Wright

Nothing in life is fun for the whole family. There are no massage parlours with ice cream and free jewellery.

Jerry Seinfeld

What's the point of going out? We're just going to end up back here anyway.

Homer Simpson, The Simpsons

I take my children everywhere, but they always find their way back home.

Robert Orben

A dedicated follower of fashion

No dad wants to appear the oldest at the school gates, but eventually there comes a time in life when you have to accept that a cheesecloth shirt, gold medallion, wrap-around shades and tight jeans are

*simply not appropriate, particularly at a parents'
evening.*

I love my dad, although I'm definitely critical of
him sometimes, like when his pants are too tight.

Liv Tyler, daughter of Aerosmith frontman Steve Tyler

My dad's pants kept creeping up on him. By 65 he
was just a pair of pants and a head.

Jeff Altman

Fathers don't wear bathing suits, they wear trunks.
It's kind of the same thing a tree would wear if it
went swimming.

Jerry Seinfeld, SeinLanguage

Your father, his idea of culture is an undershirt with
sleeves.

Marie Barone, Everybody Loves Raymond

I paid a quid for these underpants, and I've got
about fifty pence worth stuck up me arse.

Jim Royle, The Royle Family

—What the hell is that?

—A dress.

—Says who?

—Calvin Klein.

Mel Horowitz, Cher Horowitz, Clueless

I have a 16-year-old daughter. She's growing up and I don't know when it happened. I came home the other day and I'm helping my wife fold clothes. I pick up a little pair of skimpy knickers and I go, 'Hey, hey, when are you gonna wear these for me?' She goes, 'I can't. They're your daughter's.'

Bill Engvall

Paul Hennessy: Hold it, I can see your bra and that slingshot you're wearing.

Kerry Hennessy: Must be Casual Sex Day at school.

Bridget Hennessy: It's a thong.

Paul Hennessy: It's floss.

8 Simple Rules For Dating My Teenage Daughter

I have always dressed according to certain Basic Guy Fashion Rules, including: both of your socks should

always be the same colour, or they should at least
both be fairly dark.

Dave Barry

My socks *do* match because I go by thickness.

Steven Wright

You know you're getting like your dad when you
start wearing tartan slippers.

Anon

The average father cannot be trusted to put
together combinations of clothes. He is a man who
was taught that the height of fashion was to wear
two shoes that matched.

Bill Cosby, Fatherhood

Babies are much smaller than adults. As such,
attempts to dress them in your hand-me-downs will
be an abysmal failure.

Peter Downey, So You're Going To Be A Dad

When did it become socially acceptable to wear a football jersey so freely off the pitch? Does dad really have to wear it to his place of work? Especially when his place of work is a hospital.

Dylan Jones

My dad was vain and wore so much foundation that if you had punched him in the face it would have taken a couple of seconds to reach flesh.

Judith Lucy

Never wear anything that panics the cat.

P.J. O'Rourke

I just dress in what is comfortable and covers up my gut as much as possible, because the problem is that I look like a minicab driver. You know there are some of us that are just fated to look like minicab drivers. It doesn't matter what clothes you put on, or how much you pay for them, you're still going to look like a minicab driver.

John Peel, Grumpy Old Men

My dad is waiting until he loses weight before buying new clothes. So he's still wearing his Cub Scout uniform.

Rita Rudner

He Who Must Be Obeyed

Parenting books state that dads are meant to impose discipline, but these books fail to mention that a tearful look from a daughter can reduce you to jelly. So what starts out as a severe telling-off ends with a hug and a whispered: 'If Mum asks, tell her I read you the riot act.'

My father never raised his hand to any of his children except in self-defence.

Fred Allen

I hate to travel. I guess it's because my father used to beat me with a globe.

Dave Attell

My father would thrash me every now and then. He'd talk while he did it too! He'd hit me and shout, 'Have ye had enough?' Had enough? What kind of question is that? 'Why, Father, would another kick in the balls be out of the question?'

Billy Connolly

Why do parents always take their children to supermarkets to smack them?

Jack Dee

If you are allowed to smack children, you should be allowed to smack geriatrics as well because they are just as much of a nuisance as children, if not more.

Jack Dee

I'd like to smack smug parents who say, 'Our three-year-old's reading *Harry Potter*.' Yeah, well my three-year-old's smearing his shit on the fridge door.

Jack Dee

I won't have my kids getting lippy. No swearing. I don't smack either. I give them a dropped eyebrow look and then they know.

Liam Gallagher

I love my kids. I try to bring them up the right way, not spanking them. I find that I don't have to spank them. I find that waving the gun around pretty much gets the same job done!

Denis Leary

My father only hit me once – but he used a Volvo.

Bob Monkhouse

As the saying goes, if you can't beat them… what's the point in having kids?

Lee Mack

I don't understand why anybody would ever beat their children when damaging them psychologically is so much more permanent.

Tom Rhodes

When I have a kid, I want to buy one of those strollers for twins, then put the kid in and run around, looking frantic. When he gets older, I'd tell him he used to have a brother, but he didn't obey.

Steven Wright

I don't scold my baby because she's too young, she doesn't know what she's doing. But when she's 15 her ass is grounded.

Gallagher

My father used to ground me – and then run electricity through me.

Anon

Advice for when a child under four is having a tantrum is 'throw some water on them'. I tried it and my kid screamed even more. His mum said I shouldn't have used the kettle.

John Bishop

My parental tactics run the gamut from moving speeches on racial pride to outright bribery in the form of cold cash.

Bill Cosby

There are three ways to get something done: do it yourself, hire someone, or forbid your kids to do it.

Anon

—I don't care what your story is. The rule is you call.

—It was a rough neighbourhood. When I finally found a phone booth, I got tired of waiting for the guy in it to finish peeing.

Dan Conner, Darlene Conner, Roseanne

My father was frightened of his mother, I was frightened of my father, and I am damned well going to see to it that my children are frightened of me.

King George V

—I've had a good life. And you can always be proud of your father and all of his accomplishments.

—What accomplishments?

—Go to your room.

Peter Griffin, Meg Griffin, Family Guy

When your dad is angry with you and asks, 'Do I look stupid?' don't answer him.

Anon

—I don't understand why it is that you get to rant and rave and I'm the one that has to be calm.

—Because, Cliff, that is my baby in there!

—Well, that's my baby, too!

—No, Cliff, you did not have that child. I had that child. I was the one who was lying on that table screaming, 'Take it out!'

Cliff Huxtable, Clair Huxtable, The Cosby Show

I only have two rules for my newly born daughter: she will dress well and never have sex.

John Malkovich

Until I was 13, I thought my name was 'Shut Up'.

Joe Namath

'Get down! Get down!' I thought my dad was James Brown when I was a kid.

Lee Evans

You hate to say things that will upset your kids, but then sometimes you have to because you can't let them run around wild.

Ozzy Osbourne

—Hal, this isn't funny. That behaviour isn't acceptable.
—You're right. Boys, the next time you drive a golf cart over a catered lunch and into a swimming pool there will be consequences.

Lois, Hal, Malcolm in the Middle

If a child shows himself incorrigible, he should be decently and quietly beheaded at the age of 12.

Don Marquis

My wife and I have contrasting parental styles. As a parent I'm pretty demanding. I say, 'No, no, no!' But my wife insists, 'Yes, yes, yes…we have to teach the children to talk.'

Jason Resler

When the kids have their friends round, I have to pretend to be Fun Dad so they won't go back to their parents and say: 'He was really shouty.'

Jonathan Ross

—All I wanted was to be with my friends, Dad. A lot of people I like are going to be down there.
—Christmas is not about being with people you like. It's about being with your family.

Brad Taylor, Tim Taylor, Home Improvement

My father told me never to darken his door again. It was no big deal, I just painted his door the wrong colour.

Jim Loy

Font of all knowledge

Dads are in the privileged position of being able to answer any question their children throw at them – so long as that question relates to sport, beer, music or TV. Any other subject is liable to elicit a shrug, a grunt or an 'Ask your mother'.

'What separates us from the beasts, Daddy?' a child asks his dad at the zoo. The dad replies, 'That big wall there.'

Chris Addison

One of the hardest things about being a parent is you're expected to know everything, but you realise you don't because your kids have asked you. 'Dad, how does electricity work?' 'Er, uh, you put a plug in.'

Jack Dee

When a kid asks an experienced father how much a certain building weighs, he doesn't hesitate for a second. '3,475 tons,' he says.

Dave Barry

Their homework is so hard these days. I sat down with Brooklyn the other day and I was like, 'Victoria, maybe you should do the homework tonight.' I think it was maths.

David Beckham

My daughter came home from high school the other day and said, 'Daddy, can you help me with my maths homework?' I said, 'Sure, honey, let me take a look at it... When did they start putting letters with it?'

Bill Engvall

I didn't realise how good I was with technology until I met my parents. My dad told me: 'You're good, you should be a computer programmer.' I said: 'You're bad, you should be a caveman.'

Mike Birbiglia

I have never been jealous. Not even when my dad finished fifth grade a year before I did.

Jeff Foxworthy

You know how you look up to your dad when you're a little kid like he's got some special Dad knowledge. And then you find out all he really knows is how to have sex with your mom.

Jake Johannsen

—Dad, what's the blow-hole for?
—I'll tell you what it's not for, son. And when I do, you'll understand why I can never go back to Sea World.

Chris Griffin, Peter Griffin, Family Guy

My young son asked me what happens after we die. I told him we get buried under a bunch of dirt and worms eat our bodies. I guess I should have told him the truth – that most of us go to Hell and burn eternally – but I didn't want to upset him.

Jack Handey

Jarrell was not so much a father as an affectionate encyclopaedia.

Mary Jarrell

You teach your daughters the diameters of the planets and wonder when you are done that they do not delight in your company.

Samuel Johnson

My father adored Shakespeare. Every time he caught sight of me he would say: 'Is execution done on Cawdor?' When you're four, that's a pretty tough question.

John Mortimer

You know that children are growing up when they start asking questions that have answers.

John J. Plomp

My daughter asked me, 'Daddy, what's a pronoun?' I said, 'I don't know, a noun with a job?'

Rich Vos

I told my father I was punished in school because I didn't know where the Azores were. He told me to remember where I put things in future.

Henny Youngman

Things you can learn from your kids:
- When you hear the toilet flush and the words, 'Uh-oh,' it's already too late.
- A king-size waterbed holds enough water to fill a 2,000-square foot house four inches deep.
- Super glue is forever.
- VCRs do not eject peanut better and jelly sandwiches even though TV commercials show they do.
- The fire department has at least a five-minute response time.
- The spin cycle on the washing machine does not make earthworms dizzy.
- It will, however, make cats dizzy.
- Cats throw up twice their body weight when dizzy.

Anon

You call that music?

Every generation instinctively believes that the music of their youth was the best. Consequently, even though their CD racks are full of Keane, Coldplay and Snow Patrol, many dads moan about today's music, even criticising modern bands for not having sensible names like Steeleye Span or Mott the Hoople.

My son does not appreciate classical musicians such as the Stones; he is more into bands with names like Heave and Squatting Turnips.

Dave Barry

Whoever proclaimed that a cat scratching its claws down a blackboard was the worst sound ever, had obviously never heard a dad on a karaoke night.

Anon

When I dance, people think I'm looking for my
keys.

Ray Barone, Everybody Loves Raymond

I'm with my children for a maximum of 15 minutes
a day, and this is no match for the constant
bombardment they get on Radio 1 from Sara Cox
and the Cheeky Girls. I want my eight-year-old to
be a good girl. But over Christmas I learn she wants
to be a 'teenage dirtbag baby'.

Jeremy Clarkson, The World According to Clarkson

Nothing separates the generations more than music.
By the time a child is eight or nine, he has
developed a passion for his own music that is even
stronger than his passions for procrastination and
weird clothes.

Bill Cosby

My foster daughter Tiger Lily calls me Dad. We
were shopping the other day and they played one
of my songs, then one of her dad (Michael
Hutchence)'s. She said, 'That's you, Dad.' Then

she said, 'That's my real dad. My real dad's a better singer than you, Dad.' I just said, 'Sheeesh… Thanks.'

Bob Geldof

When we started making electronic music I imagined that the reaction we got from the rock musicians must have been similar to the one the beat groups got from people like my dad.

Trevor Horn

He was like a real dad, you know. We used to sit down with guitars and mess around.

Julian Lennon

The only musical instrument most dads should be let near is the air guitar.

Anon

Michael Bolton says he now wants to become an opera singer, which is great, because now my dad and I can hate the same kind of music.

Conan O'Brien

The greatest advantage of top volume was that I couldn't hear the grownups when they came in to tell me to turn that crap down.

Bill Cosby, Fatherhood

Must we have all these things blaring at us? I start every day in a state of deep shock.

Ben Parkinson, Butterflies

—It's not junk, Dad, it's heavy metal.
—It sounds like they're banging their heads on their guitars while they're getting their teeth drilled.
—Hey, cool – you saw the video!

Randy Taylor, Tim Taylor, Home Improvement

Competitive Dad

*It's in the genes of dads to be fearlessly competitive…
as any child who has been sent straight to bed for
winning at Monopoly will testify.*

I'm gonna be the best daddy on the planet and I'm gonna enter the best daddy competition and I plan to win it!

Jack Black

Right, let's take a vote. Who gave the best presents this year?

Competitive Dad, The Fast Show

My dad's so competitive. I rang him up to boast that we had been to Downing Street and he just said: 'How ridiculous.' The Blairs were ridiculous, everything was ridiculous. Whereas, of course, if it had been he who had been invited, it would have been 'Tony this' and 'Cherie that'.

Harry Enfield

I was out watching my son, Jack, play football the other day, and he missed the goal. Tried some fancy footwork and missed. I was going nuts. I shouted at him, 'Should've gone to Specsavers, Jack!' The other dads were going, 'Ooh, nasty.' But you have to teach kids to be hungry to win.

Gordon Ramsay

Okay Marge, it's your child against my child. The winner will be showered with praise. The loser will be taunted and booed until my throat is sore.

Homer Simpson, The Simpsons

I made a vow to my wife not to take up golf until the kids have left home, or at least until they have reached that stage in their lives when they want absolutely nothing to do with me.

Dylan Jones

Father's Day must have been tough for Jesus. It'd be like, 'Uh…here, Dad, I got you this paperweight.' 'I made that!'

Jim Gaffigan

[My son] George looked at me and said: 'Wouldn't it be great to have Beckham as your dad?' I asked: 'Why would that be?' and George said: 'Because he's so good at football.'

Gary Lineker

When are you going to learn, Ray? You can't talk sports with the wife.

> *Frank Barone to his son,* Everybody Loves Raymond

Until I became a parent, I thought children just naturally knew how to catch a ball, that catching was an instinctive biological reflex that all children are born with, like knowing how to operate a remote control or getting high fevers in distant airports.

> *Dave Barry*

I had a dream last night where I was playing football with my kid, actually with him. I'm on this field, and they hike me the baby, and I've got to do something, 'cause the Tampa Bay defence is coming right at me.

> *Ross Geller,* Friends

There must be many fathers around the country who have experienced the cruellest, most crushing rejection of all: their children have ended up supporting the wrong team.

> *Nick Hornby,* Fever Pitch

My father has taken up bird-watching, and he's very serious about it. He bought binoculars. And a bird.

Rita Rudner

I think the saddest day of my life was when I realised I could beat my dad at most things, and Bart experienced that at the age of four.

Homer Simpson, The Simpsons

Son, when you participate in sporting events, it's not whether you win or lose – it's how drunk you get.

Homer Simpson, The Simpsons

I was watching the Superbowl with my 92-year-old grandfather. The team scored a touchdown but when they showed the instant replay, he thought they scored another one. I was gonna tell him, but I figured the game he was watching was better.

Steven Wright

Nobody's perfect

There are times when even the best dads in the world slip up – forgetting a birthday, momentarily forgetting your son's name or forgetting that he's been accidentally locked in the garden shed since November.

The son whines to his father, 'You messed up my childhood!' And the father says, 'How could I, son? I wasn't even there.'

Anon

When Mom got mad, she'd threaten me: 'Wait till your father gets home.' I'd say: 'Mom, it's been eight years…'

Brett Butler

—Jane. It's been a long time.
—Yes.

—How are the children?

—We didn't have any children.

—Yes, of course.

> *Frank Drebin, Jane Spencer,* The Naked Gun 2½:
> The Smell of Fear

—God, I hope you're not inviting that bloody, bollocky, selfish, two-faced, chicken bastard, pig-dog man, are you?

—You could just say 'Dad'.

> *Edina Monsoon, Saffy Monsoon,* Absolutely Fabulous

—During that period when my folks were separated, my dad went a little crazy.

—Not a very long trip.

> *George Costanza, Jerry Seinfeld,* Seinfeld

My father would say to my mother: 'Must you quarrel with me on the street? What do we have a home for?'

> *Sam Levenson*

I've got five stepmothers. My dad's been approved for a Marriage Licence Gold Card.

> *Christopher Titus*

I've got two daughters, and I was divorced when they were young – four and two. They took it bad…because I told them it was their fault.

Rich Vos

I remember turning up on his doorstep and saying: 'Hello, I am your son.' He fainted.

Antony Worrall Thompson

And my parents finally realise that I'm kidnapped and they snap into action immediately: they rent out my room.

Woody Allen

For my 12th birthday I got an electric lawn mower to do the lawn for my father. That was my present, with a bow on it and everything. Thank you very much, Dad, thank you *very much*.

Dan Aykroyd

One Christmas, things were so bad in our house that I asked Santa Claus for a yo-yo and all I got was a piece of string. My father told me it was a yo.

Brendan O'Carroll

I have an eight-year-old child, and he's a bit deranged because he's been living with me for eight years.

Jason Byrne

We're not really good parents, we're not bad parents, we're just really new parents. People always ask us, 'Are they sleeping through the night?' And we're like, 'As far as we know.'

Henry Cho

I was entrusted with the task of being a single father for two days, and frankly I'd have been better off doing underwater knitting. I made a complete hash of it. When my wife arrived home on Sunday evening, way past the kids' bedtime, one child was bleeding profusely, one had left home and the other was stuck up a tree.

Jeremy Clarkson, The World According to Clarkson

Almost all fathers drop their kids at some time or another. But not twice in two days. Judy exploded: 'You're not fit to take care of a hamster!'

Richard Madeley

I banged my baby's head getting into the van. She didn't cry – she just looked at me as if to say, 'Are you that stupid?' Then she cried.

Gallagher

Boys just make up games like they want to hurt themselves. My son came out into the backyard and said, 'Hey, Dad, throw that brick at me and see if I can get out of the way. Fling one right at my head and don't tell me. Let me judge by the whooshing sound.' Now don't you judge me because it wasn't until that brick left my hand that I thought, 'This is probably not a good idea.'

Tim Hawkins

They don't grade fathers, but if your daughter's a stripper, you fucked up!

Chris Rock

A dad is a man who expects his son to be as good a man as he meant to be.

Carolyn Coats

I come from a very large family – nine parents.

Jim Gaffigan

—This coming from the guy who once threw his shoe at a swan.

—It's called protecting your sandwich.

Ray Barone, Frank Barone, Everybody Loves Raymond

My father invented a cure for which there was no disease and unfortunately my mother caught it and died of it.

Victor Borge

I'm glad they invented emoticons, otherwise I wouldn't know what my dad was thinking.

Kerry Godliman

I make it a rule to pat all children on the head as I pass by – in case it is one of mine.

Augustus John

The first time I saw a naked woman was in a pregnancy magazine. This was a very confusing magazine for a ten-year-old boy to discover, because the women looked nothing like the women in my life. My sister did not have a huge, gigantic stomach, my mother did not have a huge, gigantic stomach, but my dad did.

Paul Merrill

Oh no! What have I done? I smashed open my little boy's piggy bank, and for what? A few measly cents, not even enough to buy one beer. Wait a minute, lemme count and make sure…not even close.

Homer Simpson, The Simpsons

You know, Mrs Buckman, you need a licence to buy a dog, to drive a car – hell, you even need a licence to catch a fish. But they'll let any butt-reaming asshole be a father.

Tod Higgins, Parenthood

Dad'll fix it

Dads pride themselves on their ability to carry out repairs around the house and will press on even if their activities have blacked out the entire neighbourhood. This determination to finish the job, come what may, means that many a father has led his daughter up the aisle on her wedding day clutching a half-repaired electric kettle in his free hand.

From watching my dad, I learned a lesson that still applies to my life today. No matter how difficult a task may seem, if you're not afraid to try it – and if you really put your mind to it – you can do it. And when you're done, it will leak.

Dave Barry

I do like a bit of DIY. I put some shelves up – did it properly, nice and straight. Then some idiot goes and puts something on them.

Jack Dee

The only person who could start our lawnmower was my father and he could do this only by wrapping the rope around the starter thing and yanking it for a weekend, requiring more time and energy than if he'd cut the entire lawn with his teeth.

Dave Barry

My mother and I once paid out for a séance in Widnes. We wanted to contact my father because we were going camping and couldn't lay hands on the mallet.

Kitty, Victoria Wood As Seen On TV

Sun shone in the morning and tempted us down to the beach. We took the windbreak and an axe, which is my father's traditional instrument for knocking the windbreak into the sand. It may save

him money on a mallet, but one does feel rather
sinister taking a wife, two small children and an axe
down to the beach.

Michael Palin, Diaries 1969–1979

When I was a kid, I used to imagine animals
running under my bed. I told my dad, and he
solved the problem quickly. He cut the legs off the
bed.

Lou Brock

Christmases were terrible, not like nowadays when
kids get everything. My sister got a miniature set of
perfumes called Ample. It was tiny, but even I could
see where my dad had scraped off the S.

Stephen K. Amos

Once, my son expressed a vague interest in building
a small Airfix aeroplane. What he meant, of course,
was that he'd like to spend a few moments watching
me trying to build such a thing before returning to
the PlayStation.

Jeremy Clarkson, And Another Thing…

These DIY stores cover 17½ acres and they seem to specialise in having everything except the one thing you went there for. There's no one to ask, because they don't employ anyone between the ages of 16 and 78, so there's no one with a full mental capacity anyway.

Jack Dee

You know you've turned into your dad the day you put aside a thin piece of wood specifically to stir paint with.

Peter Kay

Hell hath no fury like a dad whose tools are mixed up.

Anon

—This is my house, that is my dishwasher, and I will rewire it if I want to.

—No! You will not rewire it and screw it up like you did the blender.

—What is your problem with the blender? It's the only blender on the block that can puree a brick!

Tim Taylor, Jill Taylor, Home Improvement

How to be a good dad

There are no definitive rules for being a good dad, but the following nuggets of wisdom may at least help you challenge Homer Simpson in the league table.

Don't try to make children grow up to be like you, or they may do it.

Russell Baker

Baby's room should be close enough to your room so that you can hear baby cry, unless you want to get some sleep, in which case baby's room should be in Peru.

Dave Barry

Never raise your hand to your kids. It leaves your groin unprotected.

Red Buttons

I graduated with a physical education major and a child psychology minor, which means if you ask me a question about a child's behaviour, I will tell you to tell the child to do a lap.

Bill Cosby

I believe in honesty with my kids. When they say, 'Daddy, what will I be when I grow up?' I tell them, 'Disappointed.'

Hal Cruttenden

If a kid asks where rain comes from, I think a cute thing to tell him is, 'God is crying.' And if he asks why God is crying, another cute thing to tell him is, 'Probably because of something you did.'

Jack Handey

I believe in making the world safe for our children, but not our children's children, because I don't think children should be having sex.

Jack Handey

To be a successful father there's one absolute rule: when you have a kid, don't look at it for the first two years.

Ernest Hemingway

Reprimand your child regularly every day. You may not know why, but the kid does.

Harry Hershfield

The best way to stop your children being spoilt is to keep them in the fridge.

Anon

If you cannot open a childproof bottle, use pliers or ask a child.

Bruce Lansky

Just be good and kind to your children, because not only are they the future of the world, but they are the ones who can eventually sign you into the home.

Dennis Miller

A good father needs infinite patience, boundless enthusiasm, kindness, the ability to score a goal, take a wicket, and hit a winning serve, and the strength to say 'No' every now and again.

Piers Morgan

Never underestimate a child's ability to get into more trouble.

Martin Mull

We're hands-on parents. It's us and only us that drop him off at daycare and choose the nanny.

Kevin Nealon

Even very young children need to be informed about dying. Explain the concept of death very carefully to your child. This will make threatening him with it much more effective.

P.J. O'Rourke

Children from the age of five to ten should watch more television. Television depicts adults as rotten sons-of-a-bitch given to fist fights, gunplay, and other mayhem. Kids who believe this about grownups aren't likely to argue about bedtime.

P.J. O'Rourke

—You're giving a kid a cupcake in a new car? What are you thinking about?
—Baby gets a little nervous whenever I take him to the paediatrician, so I'm trying to make the whole experience a little more positive. It's called parenting, Earl.
—Oh please. I've been parenting for 15 years, nobody has to tell me how to be a good dad. You get one crumb on that seat and you're crawling home, buster!

Earl Sinclair, Fran Sinclair, Dinosaurs

Fathers should be neither seen nor heard. That is the only proper basis for family life.

Oscar Wilde

Any man can be a father but it takes someone special to be a dad.

Anne Geddes

That's so not funny

Dads are renowned for their corny jokes, so unless you've used at least one of the following, you can't call yourself a real dad:

- (To someone who says, 'I feel like a jam doughnut.') 'Funny, you don't look like one!'
- (To someone who says, 'Shall I put the kettle on?') 'Yes, if you think it will suit you!'
- (Driving past a cemetery.) 'That place is really popular – people are dying to get in!'
- (To someone who says, 'I'm thirsty.') 'Hi, I'm Friday.'
- (To someone who says, 'Dad, I'm hungry.') 'Hi hungry, I'm Dad.'
- (To someone who says, 'I'm off.') 'I wondered what the smell was!'

- (To someone who says, 'What's on the telly?')
  'Dust and a small vase.'
- (To someone who says, 'How long will dinner
  be?') 'Four inches – it's sausages!'
- (In a place with stuffed, mounted animal heads
  as decoration.) 'It must have been going fast
  when it hit that wall!'
- (To someone who says, 'Do you know the garage
  light's on?') 'No, but you hum it, I'll play it!'
- (When someone falls over their feet.) 'Did you
  enjoy your trip?'
- (Driving past black and white cows.) 'It must be
  cold out there because those cows are Friesian!'
- (To a son or daughter asking for money.) 'I'd like
  to help you out. Which way did you come in?'
- (Faced with a huge joint of meat on the table.) 'I
  don't know what the rest of you are having!'
- (To someone who says, 'Will you put the cat
  out?') 'I didn't know it was on fire!'
- (To someone who says, 'I'm just going to file my
  nails.') 'Under what?'
- (To someone who says, 'Do they serve mussels in
  this restaurant?') 'They'll serve anyone!'

- (When a fire engine rushes past, siren blazing.) 'He'll not sell many ice creams going that fast!'
- (To someone who reaches over and says, 'It's a long stretch.') 'Yes, but you get time off for good behaviour!'
- (To someone who says, 'What would you say to a nice piece of haddock?') 'Hello, nice piece of haddock!'

My dad has a weird sense of humour. You can see his jokes coming a mile off. He'll say, 'I've got a joke for you,' and they're so awful. I'll say, 'I can't tell these jokes on stage – I'll get beaten up!'

Alan Carr

Dad said to me once: 'Listen, son, one day I'll take you away from all this squalor and we'll live in Venice and ride up and down the Grand Canal on a Gorgonzola. I said: 'But Daddy, that's a lump of cheese.' He said: 'Who the hell cares as long as it doesn't leak!'

Les Dawson

—Dad, what would you say if I told you I didn't want to be in the Scouts?

—I'd say, 'Come again?' and I'd laugh as I said, 'Come.'

Chris Griffin, Peter Griffin, Family Guy

Dad always thought laughter was the best medicine, which I guess is why several of us died of tuberculosis.

Jack Handey

When I was a child and I'd fall over and cut myself, I'd come staggering in from the backyard sobbing, snot dripping down my top lip, and my dad would look at the blood on my knee or elbow and shout to my mum: 'Deirdre, go and get the saw out of the shed, I'll have to cut it off,' and then I'd start wailing like a banshee.

Peter Kay, The Sound of Laughter

'Daddy, when I'm grown up, I want to be an actor.' 'Don't be greedy, son,' he'd say, 'you can't be both.'

Hugh Leonard

I have a lot of very close girlfriends and sisters – I'm from an all female family. My father often quips that even the cat was neutered!

Shirley Manson

My dad was a joker. Whenever I misbehaved, he would bury me in the backyard – only up to the waist, but you can get real dizzy when all the blood rushes to your head.

Emo Philips

Get that door will ya, Antony, and if it's the Invisible Man, tell him I can't see him!

Jim Royle, The Royle Family

Father and son

The relationship between father and son can be notoriously tricky, as the younger man seeks to assert himself in adulthood. In a perfect world they can end up best friends, but in other cases they may fight like Tom and Jerry.

I once punched a bloke in the face for saying *Hawk the Slayer* was rubbish, when what I should have said was, 'Dad, you're wrong.'

Bill Bailey

I would have loved to have had a gay dad. Do you remember at school, there were always kids saying, 'My dad's bigger than your dad. My dad will batter your dad!' So what? 'My dad will shag your dad. And your dad will enjoy it!'

Frankie Boyle

The first time my dad saw me in lipstick he said: 'Tell me the truth, son, are you a nancy boy?'

Michael Caine

Men think about sex every seven seconds, which I think makes talking to your dad very creepy.

Jimmy Carr

—You want to establish this great father–son relationship? Well, that kind of thing takes a couple of years, not a couple of days.

—A couple of years, eh?

—Ah, it'll go by before you know it.

—Either that, or it'll seem like eternity.

Martin Crane, Frasier Crane, Frasier

—Well, I guess from now on it's just you and I.

— 'You and me', Dad.

—This is gonna be great!

Martin Crane, Frasier Crane, Frasier

I don't think my dad liked me very much because when I was seven I had wax in my ears and instead of taking me to a clinic, he stood me in a saucer and used me as a night light.

Les Dawson

A king, realising his incompetence, can either delegate or abdicate his duties. A father can do neither. If only sons could see the paradox, they would understand the dilemma.

Marlene Dietrich

I had Spartacus as my father. It was overwhelming.

Michael Douglas, on dad Kirk

My son has taken up meditation. At least it's better than sitting and doing nothing.

Max Kauffman

—Son, I just want you to know that I have total faith in you.
—Since when?
—Since your mother yelled at me.

Homer Simpson, Bart Simpson, The Simpsons

The parent who could see his boy as he really is would shake his head and say, 'Willie is no good; I'll sell him.'

Stephen Leacock

Last year on Father's Day my son gave me something I've always wanted – the keys to my car.

Al Sterling

My name is Adam. My father's name is Adam.
Having the same name as your father, it's alright
until your voice changes. My friends would always
call up, 'Is Adam there?' My father would say, 'This
is Adam.' My friends would say, 'Adam, you were so
wasted last night.'

Adam Sandler

Homer Simpson: Hey, boy! Wanna play catch?
Bart Simpson: No thanks, Dad.
Homer Simpson: When a son doesn't want to play
    catch with his father, something is definitely wrong.
Grandpa Simpson: I'll play catch with you!
Homer Simpson: Go home.

The Simpsons

My father and I had dinner tonight, and I made a
classic Freudian slip. I meant to say, 'Could you
pass me the salt, please?' But it came out: 'You
prick, you ruined my childhood.'

Jonathan Katz

Father, you are a dyed-in-the-wool, fascist,
reactionary, squalid little 'know your place', 'don't

rise above yourself', 'don't get out of your hole', complacent little turd.

Harold Steptoe, Steptoe and Son

There must always be a struggle between a father and son, while one aims at power and the other at independence.

Samuel Johnson

By the time a man realises that maybe his father was right, he usually has a son who thinks he's wrong.

Charles Wadsworth

Perhaps host and guest is really the happiest relation for father and son.

Evelyn Waugh

If there is one thing that pierces the armour of an English father of the upper classes, it is to be looked down on by his younger son. Little wonder that Lord Emsworth, as he toddled along the road, was gritting his teeth. A weaker man would have gnashed them.

P.G. Wodehouse, Nothing Serious

My father was never proud of me. One day he asked me, 'How old are you?' I said, 'I'm five.' He said, 'When I was your age, I was six.'

Steven Wright

Growing up, my father told me I could be whomever I wanted. What a cruel hoax that was! I'm still his son.

Kenny Smith

Daddy's little girl

A daughter can twist her dad around her little finger like an Italian twists spaghetti around a fork. And the same man that may be a tyrant in the office or a colossus on the sports field is usually powerless to stop it happening.

A father is always making his baby into a little woman. And when she is a woman he turns her back again.

Enid Bagnold

She was growing up, and that was the direction I wanted her to take. Who wants a daughter that grows sideways?

Spike Milligan, Indefinite Articles

I can run the country or control Alice (my daughter). I can't do both.

Theodore Roosevelt

The thing to remember about fathers is…they're men. A girl has to keep it in mind. They are dragon-seekers, bent on improbable rescues. Scratch any father, you find someone chock-full of qualms and romantic terrors, believing change is a threat, like your first shoes with heels on, like your first bicycle it took months to get.

Phyllis McGinley

You know fathers don't like to admit it when their daughters are capable of running their own lives. It means we've become spectators. Bianca still lets me play a few innings – you've had me on the bench for years. When you go to Sarah Lawrence (College), I won't even be able to watch the game.

Walter Stratford, 10 Things I Hate About You

Dad told me that I was uncommonly beautiful, that I was the most precious thing in his life and that if any randy geek laid a finger on me, he would hurt them badly in their Brut-sprinkled soft places.

Dawn French

My dad used to say I had a bum you could serve tea off.

Jennifer Aniston

My father said: 'You're too fat to be Sue Lawley.'

Fern Britton

Meg Griffin: Mom, Dad, am I ugly?
Lois Griffin: Oh of course not, sweetie!
Peter Griffin: Yeah, where'd you get a stupid idea like that?
Meg Griffin: Craig Hoffman.
Peter Griffin: Craig Hoffman said that? Well, he's a sharp kid. You might be ugly.

Family Guy

When Charles first saw our child Mary, he said all the proper things for a new father. He looked upon the poor little red thing and blurted, 'She's more beautiful than the Brooklyn Bridge.'

Helen Hayes

She got her good looks from her father – he's a plastic surgeon.

Groucho Marx

Maggie, what a great little accident you turned out to be!

Homer Simpson, The Simpsons

—Peter, you're bribing your daughter with a car?
—Ah, c'mon, Lois, isn't 'bribe' just another word for 'love'?

Lois Griffin, Peter Griffin, Family Guy

Never come out to your father in a moving vehicle.

Kate Clinton

I can't believe my dad saw us having sex. He didn't make it to one of my piano recitals, but this he sees.

Monica Geller, Friends

I fell off the bike on the Thursday before Good Friday. My daughter Rosie now calls it Crap Thursday.

Rik Mayall

There was one moment where they were riding their little ponies in Scotland and Stella said to me: 'Dad, you're Paul McCartney, aren't you?' I said: 'Yes, darling, but I'm Daddy really.'

Paul McCartney

Once I had my first hit, Dad started to introduce himself as Nancy Sinatra's father.

Nancy Sinatra

I never knew my father – my mother only knew him fairly briefly.

Patsy Stone, Absolutely Fabulous

I will not allow my daughters to learn foreign languages because one tongue is sufficient for a woman.

John Milton

All I ever heard when I was growing up was, 'Why can't you be more like your cousin Sheila? Why can't you be more like your cousin Sheila?' Sheila died at birth.

Joan Rivers

I never know what to get my father for his birthday. I gave him $100 and said, 'Buy yourself something that will make your life easier.' So he went out and bought a present for my mother.

Rita Rudner

I have three daughters and I find as a result I played King Lear almost without rehearsal.

Peter Ustinov

My unhealthy affection for my second daughter has waned. Now I despise all my seven children equally.

Evelyn Waugh

The father of a daughter is nothing but a high-class hostage. A father turns a stony face to his sons, berates them, shakes his antlers, paws the ground, snorts, runs them off into the underbrush, but when his daughter puts her arm over his shoulder and says, 'Daddy, I need to ask you something,' he is a pat of butter in a hot frying pan.

Garrison Keillor

I'll drink to that

Generally speaking, dads like to unwind with a beer…usually followed by another beer…and another beer until they reach that mellow stage where they search out the photo album to remind themselves of how their teenage kids with tattoos and nose studs once looked endearingly human.

Alcohol is good for you. My grandfather proved it irrevocably. He drank two quarts of booze every mature day of his life and lived to the age of 103. I was at the cremation – that fire would *not* go out!

Dave Astor

Without question, the greatest invention in the history of mankind is beer. Oh, I grant you that the wheel was also a fine invention, but the wheel does not go nearly as well with pizza.

Dave Barry

I only take a drink on two occasions – when I'm thirsty and when I'm not.

Brendan Behan

I know I'm drinking myself to a slow death, but then I'm in no hurry.

Robert Benchley

—Y'know I remember my father, all dressed up in a red suit, the big black boots and the patent leather belt, sneaking around downstairs. He didn't want anybody to see him but he'd be drunk so he'd stumble, crash into something and wake everybody up.

—Well, that doesn't sound like a very merry Christmas.

—Who said anything about Christmas?

> *Chandler Bing, Rachel Green,* Friends

Can I have a beer so big it hurts to lift it a little bit?

> *Paul Buchman*

—Gil, you have a good memory. Uh, was it yours or Helen's or Susan's wedding I got drunk at?

—It was all three, Dad. Congratulations!

> *Frank Buckman, Gil Buckman,* Parenthood

—Coffee, Dad?

—Why not? I'm up six times a night anyway, I might as well be alert.

> *Frasier Crane, Martin Crane,* Frasier

Do not allow children to mix drinks. It is unseemly and they use too much vermouth.

> *Steve Allen*

Some people are against drink driving, but you know, sometimes you've just got no choice: those kids have got to get to school!

Dave Attell

—I feel kinda guilty, giving Chris his first taste of beer…but you turned out OK, right pal?
—I'm gonna go get wasted.

Peter Griffin, Chris Griffin, Family Guy

I don't have a kid, but I think that I would be a good father, especially if my baby liked to go out drinking.

Eugene Mirman

Now, son, you don't want to drink beer. That's for daddies and kids with fake IDs.

Homer Simpson, The Simpsons

Whenever I got sick as a kid, my dad would warm me up with a shot of hundred-proof whisky. Never got sick again…that I can remember.

Christopher Titus

Port is the perfect drink: a combination of aphrodisiac and tranquilliser. If you don't get what you want, you aren't bothered.

Barry Cryer

—Tell me you love me, Al.
—I love football, I love beer, let's not cheapen the meaning of the word.

Peggy Bundy, Al Bundy, Married…With Children

Beer: helping ugly people have sex since 3000BC.

W.C. Fields

Love makes the world go round? Not at all. Whisky makes it go round twice as fast.

Compton Mackenzie

You're not drunk if you can lie on the floor without holding on.

Dean Martin

Every time a friend of mine has a kid, I go over to the crib and say, 'You know, I used to hold your father's head while he threw up.'

Larry Miller

People will blame anything but the booze on their upset stomach. They'll say: 'For some reason, when I got in I was sick as a pig – it must have been something I ate.' And you say: 'I bet it was that packet of crisps you had between pints nine and ten.'

Jack Dee

I always know how much I've drunk because I throw it up all over the floor, and I can see it there, plain and simple.

Jack Dee

You know you have a drinking problem when the bartender knows your name…and you've never been to that bar before.

Zach Galifianakis

I told my girlfriend last night how much I loved her, and she said that I must have been out drinking again. I asked her why she would say that, and she said, 'Because I'm your father.'

Dave George

When I read about the evils of drinking, I gave up reading.

Bob Monkhouse

Therapist: Mr Nesbitt, were you close to your father?

Rab C. Nesbitt: Not unless I could help it, otherwise I would get a boot about the melt, but I always remember the friction burns he left on the carpet when I handed over my first wage packet.

Mary Nesbitt: My God! It's weird that you can live with someone for so long but you never really know them.

Rab C. Nesbitt: Didn't you know my father was an alky?

Mary Nesbitt: Oh aye, but I didn't know you had a job!

Rab C. Nesbitt

Dad was just an emotional wreck. He was drinking a lot of the time, he was smoking a lot of pot. And because he takes certain medications, the drinking was making him…you know, he wasn't even present, really.

Jack Osbourne

Once my dad was drunk when my friend came over and he chased her round in a top hat, tailcoat and his underwear.

Kelly Osbourne

When I first went to the Betty Ford Centre, I was very surprised they didn't have a bar there.

Ozzy Osbourne

—Can I pour you a draught, Mr Peterson?
—A little early, isn't it, Woody?
—For a beer?
—No, for stupid questions.

Woody Boyd, Norm Peterson, Cheers

—Never mind Pomagne. Nothing but the best for this baby. How about the old champagne? Eh, well how much is that going to set me back?

—About 25 quid.

—'Ere y'are, there's a fiver – just get a bottle of Pomagne. Well, bloody 'ell, it's not twins, is it?

Jim Royle, Antony Royle, The Royle Family

Sometimes when I reflect on all the beer I drink, I feel ashamed. Then I look into the glass and think about the workers in the brewery and all of their hopes and dreams. If I didn't drink this beer, they might be out of work and their dreams would be shattered. I think, 'It is better to drink this beer and let their dreams come true than be selfish and worry about my liver.'

Babe Ruth

My dad was the town drunk. Most of the time that's not so bad, but New York City?

Henny Youngman

My father was never home, he was always away drinking booze. He saw a sign saying, 'Drink Canada Dry.' So he went up there.

Henny Youngman

Here's to alcohol, the cause of – and solution to – all life's problems.

Homer Simpson, The Simpsons

The older generation

If your baby is beautiful and perfect, never cries or fusses, sleeps on schedule and burps on demand, an angel in every respect, then you're a grandparent.

The best babysitters, of course, are the baby's grandparents. You feel completely comfortable entrusting your baby to them for long periods, which is why most grandparents flee to Florida.

Dave Barry

—How's Freddie?

—Oh, Frederick is fine. Oh, he sends his love. He said to thank you for the toy gun you gave him. At least what he can remember of it before Lilith smashed it to bits with a croquet mallet.

Martin Crane, Frasier Crane, Frasier

When grandparents enter the door, discipline flies out the window.

Ogden Nash

Grandparents are there to help the child get into mischief they haven't thought of yet.

Gene Perret

The reason grandchildren and grandparents get along so well is that they have a common enemy.

Sam Levenson

Dad, tell me again how when you were my age you had to walk all the way across the room to change a TV channel.

Anon

My parents have the best technology that the 1970s has to offer – they still have the hi-fi with speakers the size of a twin bed and the audio quality of a walkie-talkie.

Tim Clue

—I asked Dad to pass me a bran muffin, you know what he said to me? He said, 'What's the magic word?'
—You're kidding!
—He didn't think it was very amusing when I said 'rest home'!

Frasier Crane, Niles Crane, Frasier

There's one thing about children – they never go around showing snapshots of their grandparents.

Leopold Fechtner

My Hungarian grandfather was the kind of man that could follow someone into a revolving door and come out first.

Stephen Fry

My grandfather was a very insignificant man,
actually. At his funeral his hearse followed the other
cars.

Woody Allen

I was born when my dad was fifty. It's weird
growing up with a dad that much older than you.
We'd go to the movies and we'd both get discounts.

Gary Gulman

The only thing that's worse than walking in on your
parents making love is walking in on your
grandparents making love. That's why I no longer
eat raisins.

Zach Galifianakis

The two of you will one day bless our home with
the pitter-patter of sweet little grandchildren as ugly
as sin.

Peter Griffin, Family Guy

—Now, Rudy, what did your grandpa do to make
you all quiet?

—He said if we all sit down quietly and smile, you'll give us all a dollar by morning.

Cliff Huxtable, Rudy Huxtable, The Cosby Show

My grandfather always said, 'Don't watch your money, watch your health.' So one day while I was watching my health, someone stole my money. It was my grandfather.

Jackie Mason

When I was little, my grandfather used to make me stand in a closet for five minutes without moving. He said it was elevator practice.

Steven Wright

I'm proud of my grandfather. He shot down two German planes. Unfortunately this was in 1972, but you can never be too careful.

John Moloney

My grandfather's a little forgetful, but he likes to give me advice. One day, he took me aside and left me there.

Ron Richards

My granny was recently beaten to death by my granddad. Not as in, with a stick – he just died first.

Alex Horne

—Can we not talk about nana dying?
—Yeah, have some respect, wait till she's out the door.

Denise Royle, Jim Royle, The Royle Family

I'm at the age now where the roles reverse with my parents. I go shopping with them and it's like trying to organise little ducklings. They're wandering all over.

Jerry Seinfeld, SeinLanguage

My grandkids believe I'm the oldest thing in the world. And after two or three hours with them, I believe it, too.

Gene Perret

The simplest toy, one which even the youngest child can operate, is called a grandparent.

Sam Levenson

Things dads always say

- A little dirt never hurt anyone.
- Why? Because I said so.
- When I was your age…
- Keep your eye on the ball.
- You'll learn someday.
- It's character building.
- You don't know how lucky you are.
- I only stopped off for a quick half.
- You treat this house like it's a hotel.
- I'm not made of money.
- You don't know what hard work is.
- Go and ask your mother.
- That's better out than in.
- You won't get a good job lying in bed all day.
- Who sings this rubbish?
- Don't forget, I was young once.
- You didn't get that from me.

- Don't throw that out. It might come in useful one day.
- It's not worth doing unless you do it properly.
- Give it a little gas… Not that much! Brake! Braaake! Stop!
- I'm not asleep, I'm just resting my eyes.
- What did your mother say?

Things dads never say

- What do you want to go and get a job for? I make plenty of money for you to spend.
- You've changed enough nappies today, darling. I'll sort this one out.
- Your mother and I are going away for the weekend, so you might want to think about throwing a party.
- Here, you take charge of the remote.
- Well, I don't know what's wrong with your car. Probably one of the thingies that makes it run or

something. Just take it to a garage and pay whatever he asks.

- Well, darling, now you're 13, you can stay out as late as you want.
- There's still half a glass of wine left in the bottle – we could save that for tomorrow.
- No son of mine is going to live under this roof without an earring.
- Of course I'd rather watch a Jane Austen costume drama than *Top Gear*.
- This is so much better than the music we listened to in our day.
- That woman's skirt is far too short.
- No, I've got no problem with you dating the entire chapter of Hell's Angels.
- We had it easy when we were kids.
- Here are the keys to my new car. Go out and enjoy yourself!
- No, I insist, you have the last potato.
- What do you mean, you want to play football? Figure skating not good enough for you, son?
- For your tenth birthday, why don't you go out and get yourself a nice big tattoo?

- Don't worry, someone has to be bottom of the class.
- Father's Day? Oh, don't worry about that – it's no big deal.
- No, let's just lie here and cuddle.

Love actually

For all Dad's funny ways and irritating habits, you wouldn't swap him for the world – a new car, yes; the world, no.

A dad like you is hard to find. There are so many pubs you could be in.

Anon

The Northampton fans really loved my dad. They'd sing: 'He's got no hair, but we don't care, Graham, Graham Carr.' And I'd be going: 'That's my dad!'

Alan Carr

When you're young you think your dad's
Superman. Then you grow up and you realise he's
just a regular guy who wears a cape.

Dave Attell

—Thanks, Frasier. You know, I guess I don't say it
often enough but you're a good kid.
—Well, thanks Dad. You know, there's something I
don't say often enough…
—There's nothing you don't say often enough!

Martin Crane, Frasier Crane, Frasier

I cannot understand how I managed to cope
without getting cuddled this many times a day.

Russell Crowe

I have good looking kids. Thank goodness my wife
cheats on me.

Rodney Dangerfield

He was a great dad. Every year he got so mad when
Santa didn't bring me presents.

Homer Simpson, The Simpsons

My father's mad. He's my best friend but I've seen him dangling upside-down from the climbing frame in the garden while my little boy pulls his shirt off, and I have to say: 'Stop that, you're 78.'

Chris Tarrant

The only thing that prevented a father's love from faltering was the fact that there was in his possession a photograph of himself at the same early age, in which he, too, looked like a homicidal fried egg.

P.G. Wodehouse, Sonny Boy

I've got two wonderful children – and two out of five isn't bad.

Henny Youngman

You don't have to deserve your mother's love. You have to deserve your father's.

Robert Frost

My dad's dying wish was to have his family around him. I can't help thinking he would have been better off with more oxygen.

Jimmy Carr

My dad died when I was 19, which is a bad time for your dad to die because there's an awful lot of things you have to resolve with your parents past your teens if you've been a difficult teenager.

Robbie Coltrane

I was raised by just my mum. My father died when I was eight years old – at least, that's what he told us in the letter.

Drew Carey

My mum and dad are both dead and now I think of some of the things I wish I'd said to them, like, 'Be careful of that bus!'

Kevin Gildea

I remember when my dad died, you know. I was only six. I got loads of presents off everyone like it was Christmas. I remember wishing a couple more people would die so I could complete my Lego set. My grandma tried to explain. She said he'd gone away and he wasn't coming back. So I wanted to know where, like. She said he was very happy and he'd gone to the same place as my goldfish. So I thought they'd flushed him down the bog. I thought he was just round the U bend. I used to stuff food down and magazines and that for him to read. They took me to a child psychologist in the end because they found me with my head down the bowl reading him the football results.

Dave Lister, Red Dwarf

My dad is very cool: in fact, he's cold. He's dead.

Graham Norton

As we threw my father's ashes, the wind changed and blew them all back into our faces. Our hair, skin and clothes were covered with them, which was perhaps one of the most awful, tragicomic moments of my life.

Michael McIntyre, whose father, Ray Cameron, had
co-written Kenny Everett's TV shows from 1978–85

Someone told me I should tell my dad I love him before he dies, but what if I get the timing wrong and he lives for another twenty years? I don't think either of us could deal with the embarrassment! I'd have to kill him!

Ardal O'Hanlon

I miss his quirky ways. I miss him telling me the ins and outs of what he was having for his tea, the list of every bloody pea on his plate.

Kathy Burke

Dads don't need to be tall and broad-shouldered and clever. Love makes them so.

Pam Brown

My dad...

We all have personal memories of our own dads.

My father did not like the word 'fart'. He had a way of getting around the word and would say, 'Who whispered?' And we totally accepted the euphemism in our house until, one day, my granny said, 'Come on, David, and whisper in granny's ear.'

Dave Allen

One afternoon, when I was four years old, my father came home and he found me in the living room in front of a roaring fire, which made him very angry, because we didn't have a fireplace.

Victor Borge

The one thing I remember about Christmas was that my father used to take me out in a boat about ten miles offshore on Christmas Day, and I used to have to swim back. Extraordinary. It was a ritual. Mind you, that wasn't the hard part. The difficult bit was getting out of the sack.

John Cleese

My father carries around the picture of the kid who came with his wallet.

Rodney Dangerfield

I remember the time I was kidnapped and they sent a piece of my finger to my father. He said he wanted more proof.

Rodney Dangerfield

My father was a keen trade unionist. He insisted on a tea break on his wedding night.

Les Dawson

My dad was a schizophrenic but he was good people. I remember when I was five and he was Mussolini.

Stewart Francis

My dad was in the military. He's at that age now where his war stories and other stories have blended together, so now you don't know what he's talking about: 'One time, we were surrounded, then we ran out of ammo, then we were fighting hand-to-hand, then we started dancing, and that's how I met your mother.'

Dave Attell

When the government was besieging him, Father sat in a big chair by the fire with his bad foot on a stool, armed with a cane. Not that he used it to walk with. When visitors entered he brandished it fiercely at them to keep them away from his toe.

Clarence Day, Life with Father

My dad moved in mysterious circles, because he had one leg shorter than the other.

Richie Richard, Bottom

My dad doesn't care about his height. But I often remind him that he doesn't need as much legroom on planes as I do.

Petra Ecclestone, daughter of F1 boss Bernie Ecclestone

My father hated radio and could not wait for television to be invented so he could hate that too.

Peter De Vries

My father used to sit and stare at the TV while my mother was speaking to him – I think that's a man's way of tuning out.

Garry Shandling

My father wanted me to have all the educational opportunities he never had. So he sent me to a girls' school.

Ken Dodd

I never got along with my dad. Kids used to come up to me and say, 'My dad can beat up your dad.' And I'd say, 'Yeah? When?'

Bill Hicks

My father never slept like a baby. He slept like a piece of agricultural pumping machinery.

Griff Rhys Jones, Semi-Detached

My father was from Aberdeen, and a more generous man you couldn't wish to meet. I have a gold watch that belonged to him. He sold it to me on his deathbed.

Chic Murray

My father was quite eccentric. He once told staff not to accept faxes from India because there was a plague outbreak there.

Antonia Owen

I phoned my dad to tell him I had stopped smoking. He called me a quitter.

Steven Pearl

Loose morals and effeminacy were the two things my father abhorred and he thought the theatre epitomised them both. He said: 'Acting is no good. The women are all trollops and the men are nancies.'

Kenneth Williams

Dad never forgave me for cooking. 'A cook?' he said. 'Ponces! Cooking's a fag game.'

Gordon Ramsay

When I was born, my father spent three weeks trying to find a loophole in my birth certificate.

Jackie Vernon

My father – a sausage-skin maker from Vienna who lost everything when synthetic casings replaced real sheep bladders – would take us to restaurants, pluck the sausage with a fork and then go, 'We're leaving,' if the skins weren't real.

Ruby Wax

My father was a condom salesman with ten kids.

Marlon Wayans

My dad was a kind of father figure to me.

Alan Coren

My dad's the real babe magnet.

Prince William

Index

A former journalist and TV publicist, Geoff Tibballs has written over a hundred books on a wide variety of topics, from sport to humour, social history to television. His titles for Ebury include *The Bowler's Holding, The Batsman's Willey* and *The Ultimate Cockney Geezer's Guide To Rhyming Slang*. He is the father of two daughters, and has the grey hairs to prove it.